The End

The End
A Conversation

Alain Badiou
Giovanbattista Tusa

Translated by Robin Mackay

polity

First published in French as *De la fin. Conversations* © Éditions Mimésis, 2017

This edition copyright © Alain Badiou and Giovanbattista Tusa, 2019

Polity Press
65 Bridge Street
Cambridge CB2 1UR, UK

Reprinted 2020

Polity Press
101 Station Landing, Suite 300
Medford, MA 02155, USA

ISBN-13: 978-1-5095-3626-9
ISBN-13: 978-1-5095-3627-6

A catalogue record for this book is available from the British Library.

Typeset in 12.5 on 15 pt Adobe Garamond by
Servis Filmsetting Ltd, Stockport, Cheshire
Printed and bound in the United States by LSC Communications

The publisher has used its best endeavours to ensure that the URLs for external websites referred to in this book are correct and active at the time of going to press. However, the publisher has no responsibility for the websites and can make no guarantee that a site will remain live or that the content is or will remain appropriate.

Every effort has been made to trace all copyright holders, but if any have been overlooked the publisher will be pleased to include any necessary credits in any subsequent reprint or edition.

For further information on Polity, visit our website: politybooks.com

Contents

Apologue[1]

Giovanbattista Tusa

The beginning is the negation of that which begins with it.

F. W. J. Schelling

[. . .] [T]he 'contradiction' is inseparable from the total structure of the social body in which it is found, inseparable from its formal conditions of existence, and even from the instances it governs; it is radically affected by them [. . .].

Louis Althusser, *For Marx*

The Italian storyteller Italo Calvino always saw Paris as a symbol of an elsewhere, the foreign city.[2] In Paris, he wrote, 'I have my country home, in the sense that as a writer I can conduct part of my activity in solitude, it does not matter where, in a house isolated in the midst of the countryside, or on an island, and this country house of mine is right in the middle of Paris.'[3]

The characters in Calvino's novels and short stories often exhibit a singular combination of asceticism and obstinacy, but this is always mysteriously combined with a tenacious curiosity for human beings and their contradictory situations, their peculiarities, their singularities. In *The Baron in the Trees*, Calvino tells the story of Cosimo, eldest son of the Baron Laverse of Rondeau. Following a quarrel with his parents over his refusal to eat a plate of snails, the twelve-year-old Cosimo decides to climb to the top of the oak tree in their garden – and never to come down again.

Cosimo's parents are not particularly strict, but in spite of what is, all things considered, a benign family environment, he proves indefatigably stubborn in his insistence on following his own path, his own precise, albeit eccentric, way of being in the world.

The Baron in the Trees transports us to the eighteenth century, to Enlightenment Paris. Cosimo lives in the trees, but keeps up a fervent epistolary correspondence with Rousseau. At one point he even creates a library – also in the trees – which includes the volumes of D'Alembert and Diderot's *Encyclopedia*. And it is to Diderot that he sends his *Project for the Constitution for an Ideal State in the Trees.*

Utopia, according to Deleuze and Guattari, is the conjunction of philosophy with the ambient milieu:

> [U]topia is what links philosophy with its own epoch, with European capitalism, but also already with the Greek city. [. . .] [E]tymologically it stands for absolute deterritorialization but always at the critical point at which it is connected with the present relative milieu, and especially with the forces stifled by this milieu.[4]

Also utopian is the *paradeigma* (model) of Plato's Πολιτεία (*Republic*), a book that sets out to discuss what Plato himself defined as φιλοσοφία περὶ τὰ ἀνθρώπινα (the philosophy of human affairs), the model of a *polis* that does not exist anywhere in the world, as described in Book IX at the end of the dialogue:

> I understand. You mean [. . .] the politics of the city [πόλει] we were founding and describing, the one

that exists in theory, for I don't think it exists anywhere on earth.

But perhaps, I said, there is a model [παραδειγμα] of it in heaven, for anyone who wants to look at it and to make himself its citizen on the strength of what he sees. It makes no difference whether it is or ever will be somewhere, for he would take part in the practical affairs of that city [πόλει] and no other.[5]

Philosophical engagement is a strange sort of engagement: or rather, according to Alain Badiou, one that creates a strangeness or an estrangement. It is not the same as political engagement or civil engagement precisely because it is marked by this inherent strangeness.

Truth – which, for Badiou, is axiomatic and generic, foundational – posits its own conditions of possibility. They cannot be deduced from any premise, and are not to be confused with the mere coherence, correspondence, or verification found in ordinary logics. For Badiou, the notion of truth surpasses that which can be proved or demonstrated. It cannot be deduced: philosophy must recognize and declare its existence.[6] Revolution, Badiou writes, is that which takes another turn around – it is not an absolute beginning, but something that is swept up in the spiral of a new cycle. I believe the present must be represented as a declaration of being swept up, of that which is effectively swept up in the projection. The declaration – to use Mallarmé's word, perfectly appropriate here – is the coextension of repetition and projection in this being-swept-up.[7]

In a certain sense, Badiou comes back to the notion of the authenticity of decision as detachment, as interruption of the anonymous continuum of Heidegger's *das Man*. As described in *Being and Time*, *das Man* – 'the They' – is everyone in general but no one in particular. Although the very subject of the enunciation may include himself in it, it is never assignable to a concrete circumscribed reality that could possibly be opposed.

For Badiou, it is such an interruption that instigates the tearing [*déchirure*] involved in the passage from generic animal to subject. If there is no ethics 'in general', he writes,

that is because there is no abstract Subject, who would adopt it as his shield. There is only a particular kind of animal, convoked by certain circumstances to *become* a subject – or rather, to enter into the

5

composing of a subject. That is to say that at a given moment, everything he is, his body, his abilities – is called upon to enable the passing of a truth along its path. This is when the human animal is convoked [*requis*] to be the immortal that he was not yet.[8]

In his book on Saint Paul, Badiou evokes a secularized formal conception of *grace*. Grace, 'affirmation without preliminary negation', is not a moment of the Absolute. Paul's position is radically antidialectical, and 'death is in no way the obligatory exercise of the negative's immanent power'. Rather, grace is a pure encounter, and the whole point for Badiou is to know 'whether an ordinary existence, breaking with time's cruel routine, encounters the material chance of serving a truth, thereby becoming, through subjective division and beyond the human animal's survival imperatives, an immortal'.[9]

Subjects are 'points' of truth, *local* occurrences of truth processes, particular and incomparable inductions. And, for Badiou, such a subject

goes beyond the animal (although the animal remains its sole foundation [*support*]), [and] needs something to have happened, something that cannot be reduced to its ordinary inscription in 'what there is'. Let us call this *supplement* an *event*, and let us distinguish multiple-being, where it is not a matter of truth (but only of opinions), from the event, which compels us to decide a *new* way of being. Such events are well and truly attested: the French Revolution of 1792, the meeting of Héloïse and Abélard, Galileo's creation of physics, Haydn's invention of the classical music style . . . . But also: the Cultural Revolution in China (1965–67), a personal amorous passion, the creation of Topos theory by the mathematician Grothendieck, the invention of the twelve-tone scale by Schoenberg . . . .[10]

The event is in a paradoxical position, then: it is situated, but at the same time it is also disconnected from all rules governing the situation.

At the very heart of every situation, as the foundation of its being, there is a '*situated* void': the event names the void 'inasmuch as it names the not-known of the situation'. As in the famous example that goes by the name of 'Marx', who

is an event for political thought because he designates, under the name 'proletariat', the central void of early bourgeois societies. For the proletariat – being entirely dispossessed, and absent from the political stage – is that around which is organized the

Image from the film *Tout va bien* by J. L. Godard and
J. P. Gorin

complacent plenitude established by the rule of those
who possess capital.[11]

Finally, Badiou concludes, 'the fundamental ontological characteristic of an event is to inscribe, to name, the situated void of that for which it is an event'.[12]

Heidegger's *Abbau*, Heidegger's great 'deconstruction', is the disassembling of that which has been built on the beginning: in one and the same gesture, it weakens the edifice of the metaphysical tradition and founds the historical self-positing of this tradition, carrying philosophy to its extreme, to its extremities – to its *confines*, we might say.

According to Badiou, in 'situating himself in a coming beyond of philosophy, a 'thinking thought' [. . .] that will transcend the philosophical disposition',[13] Heidegger places philosophy under a more essential determination than itself: from the Heideggerian perspective, philosophy is destined or sent by a more originary and more essential disposition of thought than philosophy itself. The destiny of philosophy, and its capacities, must always be measured against that condition which is more profound and more decisive than it itself can ever be. The overarching idea of the great Heideggerian deconstruction, according to Badiou, is 'that metaphysics is historically depleted, but that what lies beyond this depletion is as yet unavailable to us'.[14] Philosophy thus remains imprisoned, 'caught between the depletion of its historical possibility and the coming without concept of a salvational turnabout [*retournement salvateur*]. Contemporary philosophy combines a deconstruction of its past with an empty wait for its future.'[15] 'My basic intention', as Badiou writes laconically in *Conditions*, 'is to break with this diagnostic'.[16]

Image from the film *Tout va bien* by J. L. Godard and
J. P. Gorin

Tout va bien, a French film written and directed
by Jean-Luc Godard and Jean-Pierre Gorin and
which came out in 1972, depicts a factory strike
in a post-May-'68 France, complete with a picket
and imprisonment of the boss. Alain Badiou sees
it as 'an allegory of *gauchisme* on the wane', a
narration of the events that unfolded between
1969 and 1972, the political appraisal of an end,
or even, as he insists, 'the end of a beginning'.[17]

In a certain sense, Godard's film asks what conditions must be in place in order for the new to
emerge, in order for the world to be changed by

J. L. Godard and J. P. Gorin's *Tout va bien*

the experience of popular struggles. For Badiou, it is the story of a veritable re-education of a petit-bourgeois artist and a young woman through revolt and love.

And such 'is the declaration of Godard's film [. . .] in its strange, timeless beauty', he writes: 'Tout va bien' is 'the attitude of those who organize themselves freely and are answerable to no one but themselves'.[18]

The End
A Conversation

Alain Badiou
Giovanbattista Tusa

Many thanks to Isabelle Vodoz for her hospitality, and to Armel Hostiou for his images of the Conversation.

Prologue

And the Stranger, clothed in his new thoughts, acquires still more partisans in the ways of silence.

Saint-John Perse, *Anabasis*

GIOVANBATTISTA TUSA: It all begins in darkness and adversity. We recognize the scene. One man is telling the story while others listen. It's the story of Plato's cave again. This story of prisoners, of *ascesis*, and of phantoms is well known – but we will tell it again.

A number of captives are chained up in a subterranean cavern, their heads fixed facing the wall opposite the entrance, unable to see anything other than this wall. It is lit up by the reflections of a fire burning outside, midway beneath which there runs a path flanked by a low wall. Behind this wall people file by, carrying on their shoulders a motley assortment of objects, statues of men and animals. All that the captives can see of these objects is their shadows, projected by the fire onto the back wall of the cave. Similarly, all they hear are the echoes of these bearers' conversations. Accustomed since birth to watching these empty images and hearing these confused sounds, utterly ignorant of their source, the prisoners live in a world of phantoms, which they take for realities. But then, suddenly, one of them is freed from his chains and dragged towards the light. At first he is completely bedazzled. The sunlight pains him, and he can make out nothing of his surroundings. Instinctively he turns towards the shadow where his eyes can find respite from the pain. Little by little, however, his eyes become accustomed to the light, and he begins to be able to see the reflections of objects in water. Later, he feels ready to look at them directly. Finally, he can endure the sunlight. It is then that he realizes that his former life was nothing but a dark dream, and begins to pity his former fellow prisoners. But if he were to go back down to teach them, to show them the deluded

state in which they live and to describe to them
the world of light, even the wisest of them would
treat him like a madman, and may even threaten
to kill him should he persist.

The end of the story is just as well known,
and, you, Alain, also retell it in your own version
of *Plato's Republic* – but you set it in a gigantic
movie theatre. As everyone knows, in the end the
escapee will return to his fellow prisoners, back to
the shadowy cave.[1]

But I wanted to read what you wrote in your
'translation' of Plato:

The escaped prisoner's anabasis into the mountains
and his contemplation of the mountain peaks is the
Subject's ascension into the realm of thought. These
analogies, my young friends, correspond to what I
hope is true and to what you're so eager to know
about. Only from the point of view of the Other,
not of the individual – that paltry thing, even were
he Socrates – can it be determined whether my hopes
are justified. All I can say is that everything that ever
appeared to me, regardless of the time or place of
the experience, was set out in accordance with a
single principle governing its appearance. At the far
limits of knowledge, almost beyond its scope, is what

I improperly call the Idea of Truth – 'improperly', since I already told you that Truth, because it underpins the ideality of every Idea, could not itself be an Idea like the others. That's incidentally why it's so hard to construct a concept of it.[2]

As we know, for Heidegger, the duplicity of the beginning of metaphysics and the mutation in the essence of truth are part and parcel of one and the same gesture. Heidegger's interpretation of the allegory of the cave is largely devoted to outlining two different determinations of the essence of truth at work in the text. The allegory of the cave is the story of *Paideia*. Insisting that this word is untranslatable, Heidegger offers a crude approximation with the German *Bildung*, in the old sense of the word, and an analogous approximation with the French 'éducation'. But these substitutes bear only the faintest allusion to the Platonic determination: *Paideia* is an *Umwendung des ganzen Menschen*, Heidegger says, a turning around of the whole human being.

Although the original Greek concept of truth as 'unconcealing' is still operative in the allegory of the cave, another determination of truth is also at work in it, a veritable mutation in the determination of the essence of truth. Henceforth the problem will no longer be that of seeing, but that of the exactness of vision, of correspondence, and

> this conforming of apprehension, as an *idein*, to the *idea* is an *Orthotes*, an agreement of the act of knowing with the thing itself. Thus, the priority of idea and *idein* over *aletheia* results in a transformation in the essence of truth. Truth becomes *Orthotes*, the correctness of apprehending and asserting.[3]

This mutation in the essence of truth, the mutating of 'unconcealing' into rectitude, simultaneously produces a mutation of the site of truth: truth finds itself displaced from the domain of beings into that of the human attitude to those beings.

In your *Second Manifesto for Philosophy*, you argue that Plato's problem is still ours today, namely that of 'how our experience of a particular world (that which we are given to know, the 'knowable') can open up access to eternal, universal and, in this sense, transmundane truths'.[4] The problem would therefore be that '[e]ntering into the composition of a Subject orientates our individual existence while, for Plato, dialectical conversion renders possible a just life. This "entry into truth" is what the Idea brings about.'[5]

In *Conditions* you write that, contrary to every dogma of familiarity, there can be no truth except via separation. Every truth is particular, singular and even, we might say, free of all entanglement with any form of resemblance or *adequatio*.

In this respect, the story of Saint Paul is emblematic for your work, Paul being 'himself the contemporary of a monumental figure of the destruction of all politics' who, as you have written, in 'assigning to the universal a specific connection of law and the subject, asks himself with the most extreme rigour what price is to be paid for this assignment, by the law as well as by the subject. This interrogation is precisely our own.'[6]

Vertiginous words indeed. Here the relation between the subject and the law seems to be fundamental from the beginning – along with the tenacity of a saintliness that contrasts with an experience of extreme fragility. You have written, also in your text on Paul, that

[w]hoever is the subject of a truth (of love, of art, or science, or politics) knows that, in effect, he bears a treasure, that he is traversed by an infinite power. Whether or not this truth, so precarious, continues

to deploy itself depends solely on his subjective weakness.[7]

Subject and truth. What is the nature of this obscure and precarious relation?

ALAIN BADIOU: At the outset you have raised what is truly the most difficult question of all, a question upon which, in a certain sense, the whole movement of my writings bears – first of all *Being and Event*, then *Logics of Worlds*, and then the book I'm working on at the moment, which will be called *The Immanence of Truths*. That's it, the strategic question.

Why is this question so important, and why so difficult? Because we invariably find ourselves caught up in a contradiction, thinking, on one hand, that truth has a primordial autonomy, whether as clearing or as becoming or as place, and that the subject is basically a kind of inhabitant of this sovereignty; and on the other that truth is ultimately something produced by the subject. My whole problem is how to avoid coming down on either one or the other side; and this necessarily involves maintaining that there is a kind of absolutely singular co-belonging of truth and subject; so that we can say that the subject is a figure that orients the construction of truth, but at the same time we can say that truth qua evental involves a creation of possibility that does not have the subject as its source – instead, the subject depends upon it.

From a certain point of view, the subject only occurs as subject on condition that an evental rupture has taken place, followed by an oriented labour that constitutes it as subject. But on the other hand, a truth can only be created if this post-evental establishing of the subject within the possibility of the true has indeed taken place.

You see, the really difficult thing is to work out how all of this is conceptually organized. In the end, subject/truth is a couple, but it is a couple that ultimately refers to a co-relation, and sooner or later we have to define the ontological status of this co-relation. This is the primordial work done in *Being and Event*. And the conclusion I draw there is that this co-relation between subject and truth must really be conceived of as a metamorphosis of the individual, which is a pre-subject, into the figure of a subject, a metamorphosis that is only made possible by the provocation of the event. So that, ultimately, the couple truth/

subject is that which, from the point of view of the general doctrine of being, that is to say of indistinct multiplicity, constitutes a regime of exception. Truth is an exception in regard to all encyclopaedic knowledges, and the subject is an exception in regard to the individual, in regard to the co-belonging of individual and world, or the situation.

So, the difficulty is that this exception, which is the status of truths in general – truths always come in the figure of exceptions – is an exception both to the subject and to the world situation. It is an exception to the laws of the world because there are no truths without an evental rupture, and it is also an exception to the ordinary figure that is called the figure of subjectivity, because the subject is not reducible to an individual, even if an individual is traditionally its support or what is at stake in it.

This is the reason why my interpretation of Plato's cave emphasizes a point that is usually glossed over, namely that the one who comes out of the cave is *forced* to do so. Plato says this quite explicitly: it is by no means an exit that is the result of an educative process, an exit prepared for from within the cave; no, the word, the Greek word, is the word 'Bia [βία]': he is taken out by force, he is forced to exit. In my view, what is indicated by the presence of this element of compulsion in the allegory of the cave, is the fact that the subject is an exception to the individual, and that truth is an exception to knowledge, both of these things conjointly. Truth is an exception to knowledge because it can only ever be constituted outside of the cave, which is very simply the place of ordinary knowledges; and it is an exception to the individual, because the individual is forced to exit, rather than finding his way out through some spontaneous process or one that is consistent with his own nature. This is what prompted me to introduce a new expression that applies to both subject and truth, and to speak of the 'immanent exception'.

So, it could well be said that all of my philosophical work aims to explain this expression and the paradox that it represents, since normally an exception cannot be immanent, precisely because it is an exception to the laws of immanence; and inversely, what is immanent cannot be grasped in an immediate relation to the exceptional. So, the immanent exception is what I see in the allegory of the cave. It is immanent because ultimately everything happens first of all inside the cave – that is to say that the element of exit is not prescribed by the cave, it is an element of the cave, a movement in the cave, but at the same time an exception to it.

Plato doesn't really say much about the *raison d'être* of this exception: he just lets us know that, in any case, it is forced, which means that it will not be the result of reasoning about the situation in the cave. In fact, this is what you reminded us of when you cited *Saint Paul*: that we must hold to this connection between truth and subject on the side of the subject in so far as, in a certain sense, the subject comes to itself in this figure of the immanent exception. And we must also hold to it on the side of being in so far as being is not enough for a truth to be produced; a truth also requires, in some way, the collaboration of the evental rupture.

GIOVANBATTISTA TUSA: You spoke of *Bia*, the violence of the exit, as if it were something that is not produced by the situation, but rather an entirely external, entirely exceptional violence. In his *Lessons on the Philosophy of History* Hegel says that the West is characterized by a 'going outside' (*Hinaus*), by the 'exit of life out of and above itself'. According to Hegel, it is owing to this radical difference that Asia attributes so little importance to the sea: the Asiatic peoples remain closed to the sea, but 'the West', on the contrary, consists in this exit via navigation, via the incentives of navigation. The Asiatic is characterized more by immobility and by remaining within its own territories than by a movement out of the country . . . .

ALAIN BADIOU: Yes, I understand entirely what Hegel is getting at here, only what it means is that he organizes his theory of the West as exit in such a way as to ensure that, in the end, the West will be the ultimate site of absoluteness. In truth, 'going outside' does not necessarily mean expatriation: within the space of China, which can indeed be considered as a non-maritime space, a space devoted to internal commerce, it may well be the case that there have been exits, but exits internal to this space. I can see this all the more given that, in a certain sense, Chinese poetry is a poetry that is all about exit and exile.

Obviously, it could be said that the case of the official who was sent to deepest Mongolia and who wrote a magnificent poem to complain about how far he was from everything, is not the same thing as that of the navigator who goes off on an adventure, setting sail for America. But in a certain sense it is the same thing, because exit is always relative to the internal structure of the cave, and there is no reason to think that the Western cave is, in essence, qua cave, any different from the Chinese cave.

Perhaps we could simply say that the Imperial figure, the Imperial turn taken by Western truth, that is to say the interpretation of the Western adventure in a way that ultimately grants it ascendancy over all others, has not, strictly speaking, been the Chinese adventure.

What the Chinese adventure was, up to and including Mao Zedong, was the idea that the Chinese space in itself alone was the world, and that therefore it contained very many immanent exits. After all, it would be difficult to find a more spectacular example of a revolutionary exit than the Long March. It is an even more striking revolutionary exit than the storming of the Winter Palace.

The End

And always
There is a longing to dissolve. But a lot
Wants keeping. Faith.
Let us look neither before nor behind, instead
Be cradled as though
On the lake in a rocking boat.

Friedrich Hölderlin 'Mnemosyne'[1]

GIOVANBATTISTA TUSA: The 'end' has long been an obsession of philosophy. In *Das Ende aller Dinge*, 'The end of all things', Kant poses the problem as follows:

> But that at some point a time will arrive in which all alteration (and with it, time itself) ceases – this is a representation which outrages the imagination.

> For then the whole of nature will be rigid and as it were petrified: the last thought, the last feeling in the thinking subject will then stop and remain forever the same without any change. For a being which can become conscious of its existence and the magnitude of this existence (as duration) only in time, such a life – if it can even be called a life – appears equivalent to annihilation.[2]

The 'endtime' when All will be recapitulated, at once the last in the chain or series and something that stands outside the whole series, unveils the paradoxical coincidence of all of time with the eternal, in a *duratio noumenon* of which we can have no concept. This is a thought at once terrifying and sublime (*erhaben*) in which the 'end' rhymes strangely with the beginning; in the sense not of pacification or reconciliation, but of disaster.

But it is Hegel who affirms that the site of truth par excellence is the end. He is certainly not one of those philosophers who privilege the moment of beginnings. According to Hegel, in the order of Spirit, 'the first stage is the simplest, the most abstract, the poorest', whereas what comes last is richest: 'the concrete, which contains multiple determinations within itself'.[3]

Philosophy emerges as the terminal moment of an epoch, and as its determinate negation: the negativity exerted by philosophy upon a declining epoch implies its transformation *and* the production of a *new* epoch of history. And for Hegel, this philosophy is neither prophetic nor utopian; it appears as the end and completion of the epoch, anticipating, at the level of the 'absolute realm of thought',[4] the next figure of Spirit that will emerge in history.

This, as you point out, is where the 'end' comes to be considered as a positive idea in philosophy.[5] In your *Manifesto for Philosophy* you begin with the 'end', or with completion, with the radical impasse in which philosophy seems to find itself – a philosophy rendered mute, plunged into stupefied silence by the extermination of the European Jews, philosophy as guardian of the unthinkable, the inexpressible. A philosophy which, as you write,

[o]vercome by the tragic nature of its supposed object – the extermination, the camps [. . .] transfigures its own impossibility into a prophetic posture. It adopts the sombre colours of the times, heedless that this aestheticization is *also* an offence against the victims.

The contrite prosopopeia of abjection is as much a posture, an imposture, as the bugle blaring cavalry of the Spirit's second coming. The end of the End of History is cut from the same cloth as this End.[6]

You have taken up an absolutely singular position in the contemporary philosophical landscape. In answer to those who maintain that the end of the philosophical project is inevitable, or at least that the conditions of its original mission have now been stripped of all legitimacy, or worse, forgotten, it seems that for you it remains possible, and even necessary, to develop a philosophical thinking that renounces the *pathos* of being-at-the-end, one that begins, ever anew, to set out from its own specific conditions.

In your *Manifesto* you tell us that philosophy is still possible today – and not in the form of a continual being-at-the-end. Rather, what the epoch demands of philosophy is '*one more step*'.[7] But what is this step?

ALAIN BADIOU: I would begin by saying that the question of finitude and the critique of finitude have become ever more important for me as I have developed the characteristic gestures of my philosophy, and that in all likelihood there is, between the beginning of my work and its situation today, a movement by way of which, in the end, the central question becomes that of the contradiction, the relation, between finitude and the infinite. This is a central question, and one central to truths themselves, but also the point at which we can elucidate the question we began with. I wanted to say this in introduction.

Now really, as far as the *pathos* of the end is concerned, the most striking thing is how it has created an obligation to appeal to some theory or experience (or both combined) of what we might call the figure of disaster – that is to say, the figure of what is presented in reality as a radical event, but whose substance is negation or death. The way in which I approach this problem involves extracting the concept of event, an event that can be appropriated in the figure of a truth, from this figure of disaster. In particular, this is what I did in my *Ethics*.

I believe I have shown that there is really no evental dimension to genocide, to the massacre, because it is not a proposition or a possibility. On the contrary, in and of itself it is nothing but the realization of a pre-established end, namely that Germany would only be able to accomplish its historial destiny by exterminating that which rendered negation immanent – that is to say, the Jews.

There is nothing evental in this, it did not come forth in the figure of the event, it came forth in the figure of a deadly conclusion, which, far from being a beginning, completes itself absolutely as an end. And it has always seemed to me that by constructing a position around these false eventalities, these disasters that try to present as a beginning what is really an end, in order to then draw the conclusion of an end, all one is really doing is adopting the enemy's point of view. That is to say that the doctrinaire adherent of finitude, truly the greatest doctrinaire adherent of finitude, was Hitler. It was Hitler, because all of this was carried out with the sole intention of circumscribing a totality that was at once fictive and triumphal: the structure of the Aryans, the superior race, the eternal Germany, the millenarian Germany and its Reich. It therefore seems to me extremely dangerous to continue to bow to the authority of the absolute trial this kind of catastrophe, disaster, or massacre imposes upon us, and to draw from it the conclusion of the end.

I think this was a subjective victory of the enemy himself – to have in some way rendered metaphysics, or philosophy, impossible by dint of this one deadly, catastrophic act alone. To subtract ourselves from the dictatorship of the catastrophe is, in my view, very simply to say: 'we can continue'. And I myself have always experienced, almost painfully, this whole pathos of the end, this idea that one can no longer write a poem anymore, I have always truly experienced it as the triumph of the enemy.

Finally, from this perspective, Hitler was the most important person in the twentieth century, and that's something that can't be sanctioned. But neither can we oppose it with a fiction of the same order, but a positive one. This is why I have suggested that, ultimately, the radical position consists in saying that it continues, that philosophy continues. Which may seem a rather modest, rather easy position, but in reality it is the truly radical one, because it refuses to accept the imposition of a *pathos* of completion, of the end, of the impossibility of absolute novelty, when what actually took place was a disaster, a crime. Now, opposing the crime should never mean entering into the system of norms proposed by the crime itself, namely that it was the beginning of something or that it put an end to something. On the contrary, opposing it simply means circumscribing it, in all of its deadly finitude, so as to definitively prohibit its repetition, its recurrence. All of this was very important for me because, as you can see, it is of the order of philosophy, of the speculative, and of the historical.

But it is also a personal struggle, because I always felt there was something suffocating in the victory of this theme of the end. And in its correlate, the idea that 'we have once and for all experienced absolute horror, radical evil, etc.' and that all of our thought has to be reconfigured according to this experience. All this really means is that we admit the dictatorship of the crime over thought, and this I absolutely refuse, I find its imposition upon us truly intolerable.

And today we are well aware that, under the auspices of this imposition, what has been brought back? Liberal capitalism and parliamentary democracy as the alpha and omega of human existence. After all, this is what we've been peddled as compensation for the criminalization of history by the programmes of Hitler, the Nazis, and others. I can't accept that. I am in revolt against this figure. And this leads me right away to examine closely what role is being played in this affair by the concept of the end, in its double sense of completion and closure, and also to ask myself whether, maybe, ultimately, the question of truths may precisely also be the question of the in-finite – that is to say, the question of something that is not constrained by this finitude that has historically been imposed upon us.

This gives some sense of the personal journey of my relation to finitude, to the end, and to the methodology that insists on grasping the act that occasioned the disaster as if it were the obligatory point of departure for any new thought, when, if that really were the case, then this thought would precisely not be anything new. Such thinking is itself the immanent deployment of a great misfortune and, as such, it must be refused.

GIOVANBATTISTA TUSA: In your 1986–1987 seminar on Heidegger, which you were working on at the same time as *Being and Event*, you return to the Heideggerian syntagm of the 'destruction of the earth', which appears in the 1935 *Introduction to Metaphysics*. As you will recall, Heidegger's verdict is pitiless:

The spiritual decline of the earth has progressed so far that peoples are in danger of losing their last spiritual strength, the strength that makes it possible even to see the decline (which is meant in relation to the fate of 'Being') and to appraise it as such. This simple observation has nothing to do with cultural pessimism – nor with any optimism either, of course; for the darkening of the world, the flight of the gods, the destruction of the earth, the reduction of human beings to a mass, the hatred and mistrust of everything creative and free have already reached such proportions throughout the whole earth that such childish categories as pessimism and optimism have long become laughable.[8]

Heidegger opposes this darkening of the world with an appeal to confront it head on. Europe, gripped 'in the great pincers between Russia on the one side and America on the other', and especially Germany, 'standing in the centre', must recentre itself, must rediscover its proper place, or even refound it.

In your *Seminar* you emphasize a reading that brings in a political dimension of the human and of the human's relation to the earth, in so far as the idea of the earth implies the idea of the appropriation of man to his place. Heidegger's man, you say, 'has the earth as homeland, homeland in the sense of the root, the site, that which constitutes his pairing with being, that which binds him to nature qua disposition of being. Natural homeland or nature as homeland'.[9]

Heidegger's allergy to expatriation seems to go violently against the suggestion we get from Nietzsche in his reconstruction of the birth of philosophy, that of the philosopher as 'an immigrant arrived among the Greeks', an unlanded stranger . . . .

ALAIN BADIOU: First of all, I think this metaphorical figure of 'Earth' concedes too much to the poem. It concedes too much, I would say, to the representation of the 'there is', in a figure that is actually already metaphorical, already closed down, in a certain sense, in the name of 'Earth', this 'Earth' which, ultimately, will also provide the occasion for localization, for an intense vision of the original site, etc. I can't help but think of Marshal Pétain's phrase: 'The earth does not lie.' Whenever I see 'Earth' crop up, I am a little wary of the metaphorics that orchestrates all of this, even in deep ecology, metaphysical ecology.

But above all I think that the concept of 'Earth' as used here is a kind of restriction of the 'there is' to a metaphorical donation that seems potentially sacred, meaningful, open, which brings together humanity on its soil, but which in reality is the negation of a thesis I hold to be fundamental, namely that there is an infinite multiplicity of worlds, and that 'Earth' is probably an unfeasible totalization. In *Logics of Worlds*, one of the very first sentences says precisely that it is not possible to totalize the figure of worlds. There is no total universe that is representable as the original site of the 'there is' or of experience. The 'there is', qua grasped in pure multiplicity and in the multiplicity of worlds, is always fugitive.

In 'Earth' I sense the idea of a stabilizing metaphor which, in turn, allows us to speak of the devastation of 'the Earth' as of a kind of sacrilege against the originary 'there is', when the truth is that man is typically the nomad of worlds.

Indeed, we might almost define the human animal as the animal that crosses through more worlds than any other; and this multiplicity is consubstantial with it. On this point I think that we must avoid any kind of metaphorical sacralization, unless it is a matter of poetry, that is to say unless what is at stake is working within the language of singular nominations that metamorphose identities. Because poetry makes use of these kinds of things, the earth, the sky, the stars, the night, etc. But it uses them in a way that involves summoning language to use these metaphors to say of identities something more than identity itself.

A poem is always something that probes language until language, which is always charged with speaking identities, speaks them otherwise, shows that they are other than they are, or shows that they are more than they are, etc. And in fact, what the poem always tries to do is to extract the excess of each thing over itself rather than just writing its phenomenal, ordinary 'there is'. I see this as an entirely legitimate enterprise. This is a role the poem can play. But philosophy must not conceptualize this. In Heidegger there is a tendency to conceptualize the poem. But the poem is not made to be conceptualized. The poem is its own truth, and its totalizing conceptualization in the Heideggerian sense – that is to say, when the poem is seen as the ultimate task of the shepherd of Being – is a denaturing of the poem itself. This can be demonstrated quite precisely through the use of examples. We can show that what Heidegger says about poems is not what the poem intends to say in the saying itself, but something else entirely.

As for me, I distance myself from all this terrestrial logomachy, and I basically assume two antithetical, apparently dialectical statements.

On one hand, there is an infinite multiplicity of nontotalizable worlds, and therefore there is no 'there is'. On the other hand, as a general rule, in every world apart from atonal or lost worlds, there is a point of inexistence. So, on one hand there is no totality, and on the other, the way in which something is in a world is essentially punctual – namely, the figure of the minimum, the figure of that which supports the world. Not because it is the totality, but, quite on the contrary, because it is almost nothing, because it is that which is treated as the almost-nothing of the world, and it is from the almost-nothing of the world that, in truth, the testimony of the event can be born. And then, obviously, every event will be that which grasps this nothing, by lending it the possibility of being more than nothing.

And this is why I say finally that all of this is already to be found in the *Internationale*: *We are nothing, let us be all.*

GIOVANBATTISTA TUSA: Throughout your work, poetry has been of particular importance.[10] According to you a truth is never homogeneous with the dominant language of the place in which it was created, and poetry, like mathematics, expresses a limit.

In this sense, I can understand why, in your writings and your seminars, you have always attributed a decisive importance to poetry. As you wrote recently, poetry is

> the artistic form, the naive form (but here 'naivety' means 'pure invention in language'), the formal form, and the non-arrogant form, of antiphilosophy. All the more so today in that we have been the contemporaries of what I have called 'the age of poets', where a sort of agreement was reached on the fact that, systematic metaphysics being over, devalued, finished, the poem alone was the guardian of a thought for our time that would be total and yet free of philosophical pretention. The great poet Fernando Pessoa called this thought 'metaphysics without metaphysics'.[11]

But according to you, 'the age of poets has come to a close'.[12] We must instead return to Plato, that is to say to a 'clarified and primordial rearticulation of the scientific and political conditions of thought'.[13]

This is a different path than that trodden by Heidegger, who 'install[s] us in the premonition of being as beyond and horizon, as maintenance and opening-forth of being-in-totality'.[14] A path whose starting point is no longer the situational angst of the void, or what Heidegger calls 'the concern for being', 'the ecstasy of beings',[15] the great path of the poem, which seeks to reinstate the lost language of the origin . . . .

ALAIN BADIOU: In poetry it is absolutely clear that the real potential of the poem lies in its piecing together a certain saying that is manifestly the saying of that which cannot be said. So, there is always an uncertain balance between the said and the unsaid, brought together by the poem into the figure of a saying, which is in reality a possible presentation of the unsaid, without being the saying of it in the strict sense. The saying of the unsaid makes no sense, and yet that is what the poem strives for, like a threshold between saying and the unsaid. And I think it is in relation to this that all creative human activity is caught up in the paradox of being at once immanent and delinked from this immanence. All of this is extremely interesting to me because creative activity is carried out with the materials available within the world, within the situation – How else could it be done? – and yet this availability must touch upon something which, being post-evental, absolute in a certain sense, transcending the situation itself, is nonetheless created entirely within the situation. Which is the exception.

So, we come back naturally to the immanent exception, and the immanent exception is also this dialectic of subtraction – that is to say, the fact that the proper essence of a thing is not so much the intensity of its presence as the figure of that which is fugitive yet which it nonetheless manages to retain, to hold on to somehow.

GIOVANBATTISTA TUSA: 'Ending' and 'beginning'.[16]

In one of your seminars given in America, later published under the title 'Destruction, Negation, Subtraction',[17] you discuss Pier Paolo Pasolini's famous poem 'Victoria', a poem that stages the absence of all hope on the part of the dead communist partisans, as well as the perceived absence of any future on the part of the generation that came after the Second World War. For you, this poem of Pasolini's is a 'manifesto' of true negation.[18]

In Search of a Lost Real finds you reading *The Ashes of Gramsci*, another extraordinary poetic work of Pasolini's, as a testimony of the renunciation of that optimism that places its faith in a progressive path towards emancipation present in the movement of history itself. Only historic destruction on a grand scale could have been worthy of such a History: for if 'History must give birth to an emancipated world, one can without pangs of the soul accept, and even organize, a maximal destruction.'[19]

As you have emphasized many times, in the twentieth century it was negation that produced affirmation, just as destruction engendered construction. This is a conviction rooted in the twentieth century, one that

> gives to revolutionary enthusiasm its tinge of wanton ferocity: the real principles of the emancipated world surge forth from the destruction of the old world. But this is inexact, and because of this inexactitude disproportionate emphasis is placed on the destruction of the old world, and the struggle to get to the

end of this old world so as to extract from it the principles of a new one, becomes infinite, interminable.[20]

Destruction and purification as the guiding thread of the century. But already in *Being and Event* you showed how a subtractive thought of negativity can overcome the imperative of destruction and purification. The obsession of the century, moreover, was a necessary destruction, a generative destruction without which the new would never come to pass,

> because destruction does not produce the definitive, which means that we are faced with two very distinct tasks: to destroy the old, and to create the new. War itself is a non-dialectical juxtaposition of appalling destruction, on the one hand, and the beauty of victorious heroism, on the other.[21]

To such historical destruction based on an endless antagonism between the new and the old, you oppose an affirmation that also finds its starting point in negation. In the century of the 'passion for the real',[22] the avant-garde is that which proclaims a formal rupture with what preceded it, and presents itself as wielding a power of destruction of formal consensus which, at a given moment, defines what deserves the name of art.[23]

As you write, art, and so-called avant-garde art in particular, offers us a different view of the couplet destruction/subtraction. Or what, in reference to Kasimir Severinovich Malevich's painting *Black Square on White Ground* (1915), you call 'the origin of a protocol of subtractive thought that differs from the protocol of destruction'. *Black Square on White Ground*, you argue, is

> the epitome of purification. Colour and form are eliminated and only a geometrical allusion is retained. This allusion is the support for a minimal difference, the abstract difference of ground and form, and above all, the null difference between white and white, the difference of the Same – what we could call the vanishing difference.[24]

In the course of a strange and winding voyage, you have travelled through Hegel's separation, Mao's contradiction, and Marx's class struggle, only to end up (or perhaps not – this is my question) with multiplicity, mathematics. And with militant, practical fidelity to 'local' situations, each generated by an event, rooted in the actions of militants, which, in this sense, seem to be the real foundation of truth.

ALAIN BADIOU: For me, the fundamental experience of the last century, one that was already gestating in the nineteenth century, was a realization that the essence of history, and therefore of all creation, belongs to the register of the Two – that is to say, the register of a central antagonistic contradiction around which everything revolves. All other elements fall into place around this central contradiction, which is the source of everything you have just covered in your questions – the decisive importance of war as a figure, the axiom 'construction is born of destruction' – in short, the primacy of the negative, which is really a part of Engels's legacy, along with many other gestures, including in the aesthetic and even scientific avant-gardes. Because what I found striking was that, if we take the mathematical enterprise of Bourbaki in France, and indeed the creation of modern mathematics as a whole, it was also like this: locked in struggle with the old academic tradition of mathematics, one opposes to it an absolutely new, monumental construction, a system that is axiomatized through and through, etc. So, this idea, this essential idea, penetrated into all spheres.

Now I think that we're entering into a period where we absolutely must be aware that the essence of creative processes always involves three terms, and not two. This is fundamental. Not three terms in the sense of the caricature of dialectics (thesis, antithesis, synthesis), but three dialectically interrelated terms.

The clearest example of this point, after all, is politics. For a whole century, politics consisted in saying that the essence of the political was the organization of antagonism. As a consequence, the party of the proletariat was conceived at all levels as a war machine against the bourgeoisie, and consequently it was induced to fuse with a state. Once victory was assured, the party and the state, the party and power, fused into one single term so as to maintain duality at any price: on one side the party state, on the other the adversaries, the enemies, the bourgeoisie, who are still very much there, hence the at once suspicious and terroristic aspect of the enterprise.

In reality, symmetrically, we could say that the great contradiction is that between the masses and the state. Then we could say that the only valid political category is the movement qua mass movement, and that on the other side we have ossified, established power, the old world, and so on.

What I would say is that, politically, the figure of the Two has been upheld in both the tradition of the Bolshevik party and the movementist, anarchizing tradition.

One of the most interesting outcomes of this story is that, in the politics – let's say the 'revolutionary' politics – of the entire previous sequence, the thesis of the Two, as the organic thesis of political struggle, something that in truth is rooted in the vision of class struggle as primordial antagonism, was defended not only by the partisans of centralized authoritarian organization, but also by the anarchist partisans of the mass movement.

In the first case you had the party fusing with the state, in opposition to all of its enemies. And in the second case you had the revolting masses rising up against all forms of power and organization. Now, I think that the concrete history shows that we absolutely must bring in the fact that there are always three terms. For there is always a pole of exposed power, which may be the bourgeois state, but could also be the socialist state.

There is the movement because, in spite of everything, we can see very well that without a movement there can be no politics – politics just gets replaced by management pure and simple, because there is no meaningful popular scrutiny of the decisions taken. And then there is also, necessarily, a principle of organization. This principle of organization must not fuse with the state, because if it were to do so, the pure Two would reappear in the figure of the terrorist. Neither must it be identical to the movement, for the very simple reason that the movement is in its very essence something that begins and ends. So, it is something that creates a possibility, but it is not the management of that possibility, or the becoming of that possibility. So, I hold that in the field of politics, we can see very clearly that there are three terms, and that everything depends upon the articulation of these three terms. For example, will the organization, whatever it may be, prove capable of resisting any partial fusion with power, with the state, will it resist being reabsorbed, one way or another, into the always precarious historicity of movements? The organization will thus represent or draw the consequences of the movement in relation to the state.

It's a very complex question, but absolutely central today. For me, the great historical movement of the rehabilitation of Marxism, the reorientation of communism, is – to put it abstractly – the replacement of a binary dialectics with a dialectics of three terms. And this is truly a lesson to be drawn from the failure of the socialist states.

Why did the socialist states fail? Because they weren't able to move on to the next stage. They simply conserved what they had for as long as they could, up to the point where they succumbed, that's what happened. All the same, they achieved something that had never before in history been achieved: they abolished the regime of private property; but then they clung on to this abolition, until finally they let go and restored private property. And all of this because party and state were the same thing, and party and state did not admit the possibility of there being something else that would be of the order of politics. Now, if you want to regard the political phase as what Marx called the withering away of the state, that is to say the phase where the common interest has taken control, but without its taking on the form of a separate machine over and above civil society, then throughout this period there must be three terms. The state is there, of course. It's going to wither away, but for a lengthy historical period it is still there. The movement must be possible, and the state must not be in any position to hinder it, to prohibit any movement in the long run. And the organization is there, precisely as enduring institutional protection for the possibility of the movement, against the initiatives of the state.

This dialectic with three terms must constantly circulate in such a way as to create a temporality that will really be the strategic temporality. Ultimately, upon close examination, today the generic structure of truth procedures, all things considered, always involves the replacement of duality with a triplicity that is not successive but immanent. And this is why I would say that we are entering the reign of the trinity. Because it's very similar to what the Trinity meant, abstractly, on a transcendent and religious level. Basically, we can see how Father was the state, the Son was the movement, and the Spirit was the mediation between the two. The Christians knew all of this already . . . .

GIOVANBATTISTA TUSA: As André Bazin emphasized, '[d]eath is surely one of those rare events that justifies the term [. . .] *cinematographic specificity*'.[25] Technologies of the image bring us to the very heart of a 'crisis of death'. In cinema, what is impossible to capture within the field of the frame is precisely, as Lacan said, *the impasse of formalization*, that which does not participate in this work of death that cinema renders intelligible. As you emphasize in your *In Search of the Lost Real*, 'the real of a cinematographic image is that which is off-screen. The real potential of the image comes from the fact that it is deducted from a world that does not appear in the image, yet helps construct its force.'[26]

You have said that democracy and totalitarianism 'are the two epochal versions of the accomplishment of the political, according to the double category of the social bond and its representation',[27] and in general, politics is philosophically described in terms of the concept of the communitarian bond and its representation in some authority.

The task would therefore be for us to orient ourselves towards that point of the impossible where the bond is undone, where the bond no longer conditions us, no longer binds us, not even to the irreducible illusion 'of the familiarity, the resemblance, of the close [one]'. Is there only truth, as you have written, when 'the infinite at last escapes the family'?[28]

ALAIN BADIOU: Here we are dealing with a particular case, or rather, ultimately, a particular illustration, of the immanent exception, of that which constitutes the invisibility point of the visible.

Of what is the off-screen the representation? The off-screen is the representation of the fact that the force of the image qua visible is partially a result of what it has circumscribed as invisible, but precisely inside the image. So, the image is a cutout in that which otherwise summarizes, in its absence, the very place of which it is the image. And this interests me in so far as this is a subtractive dialectics that consists in locating the force of something not just in its potential for presence, but in its internal subtraction, which organizes its regime of existence, its closure, its delimitation, etc.

Art is obviously a privileged field for dealing with this because, in art, there is almost always, in the saying, a power of the unsaid. In the visible, in the circumscribed of painting, there is something of the order of absence, which structures representation itself. In cinema there is the off-screen, which delimits the presence of the image, etc.

This is the question of the real as undiscover-able, as always missing. It's the question of the event as the creation of a possibility but one that, in a certain sense, goes missing at the same time as it creates this possibility. What is directly posed here is the question of delinking – that is to say, the fact that every relation is supported by that which, within it, is not really linked, is effectively not constituted as a relation of any kind. And I think that this is where the subject is constituted: it is always the result of this operation of a dispar-ity between effective possibility and that which conditions this possibility while itself remaining absent, unrepresented, unrepresentable, mar-ginal, delinked, etc., and ultimately subtractive.

Which is why you are perfectly right, in your question, to move from the question of montage in cinema to the question of negation and non-negation in Pasolini.

These are themes which, for my part, I would address in relation to my conviction that what constitutes the presentification of the true is in reality always of the order of the delinked or subtractive, but not of the order of negation in the usual sense of the term, that is to say exclusion. It is inclusive. It is a protocol for the inclusion of that which originarily does not exactly belong to that which is included. In the end, to sum up all of this, anything of any significance that is constructed and has a universal value in a determinate situation, touches upon the *inexistent* point of that situation.

GIOVANBATTISTA TUSA: 'The inexistent'. It appears, impromptu, in *Logics of Worlds*. Allow me to cite your phrase: 'The maximally true consequence of an event's (maximal) intensity of existence is the existence of the inexistent.'[29]

A veritable subversion of being, the inexistent undermines by force of nullity that which seemed to ensure the cohesion of the world.

As you write in *Being and Event*, there is a paradox within the event itself, since the paradox of an evental site is that it can only emerge on the basis of that which does not present itself in the situation where it itself is presented. Each event is the ruin of the situation, in so far as 'every event, apart from being localized by its site, initiates the latter's ruin with regard to the situation, because it retroactively names its inner void'.[30]

You also speak of 'the inexistent' in *The Rebirth of History*, in the context of the revolts that recently swept many Arab countries. In them, what did not yet exist seemed to count for more than anything that was already manifest. More than safeguarding some order or other, it seemed that the task of insurgent political organizations was to safeguard a disorder that would not allow itself to be turned back into some consolidated state of affairs. But which nonetheless would enable the awakening of a History that does not yet exist, or did not exist.

I ask you the question that, in fact, you asked yourself at the time: 'How are we to be faithful to changing the world *within the world itself*?'[31]

ALAIN BADIOU: I am also anti-totalitarian, but in my own way. Fundamentally, the inexistent is that which, in the world, is closest to something like a pure existence, that is to say an existence reduced to existence alone, or the existence of existing. But this is a category proper to each world. Each world has that which, in itself, expresses what it is to exist in that world, but expresses it to the minimum – that is to say, at the very level of existence qua pure existence, not the distinct existence of this or that . . . .

This would be the nodal point of existing as such, and this point is on the borderline of belonging. We can link this to the question of belonging. The nodal point belongs as little as possible, as the great examples show, including political examples: take for instance the Marxist definition of the proletariat. As everyone knows, it revealed the inexistent of the political situation. And, indeed, this is the reason why the proletariat is revolutionary potential in person. But there are many other examples of the nodal point.

Today it might be, in part, the status of the nomad, or of the refugee. We can see very well how the status of the nomad or the refugee insinuates itself into consciousness as something that exists but should not exist, or that exists without existing, or exists at a minimum. And this, obviously, lies at the source of a whole series of major political disagreements. Because – and this is very important – it is always around an inexistent that a situation divides in the most violent way.

GIOVANBATTISTA TUSA: As you know, over the last few years the word 'community' has become central to philosophical debate. And yet humanity has displayed an extraordinary capacity to destroy in the name of community, to transform the very value of 'human' community into organized extermination.

The founding capacity of community, its productive or autoproductive capacity, seems to transform into its opposite: an unbridled capacity for self-destruction. In spite of everything, the community continues to be the site where self-construction and self-destruction are linked.

As you are well aware, Jacques Derrida always refused to speak of community . . . .

ALAIN BADIOU: If I may: I support him in this perspective, I am close to him on this.

GIOVANBATTISTA TUSA: . . . Derrida had a problem with the word 'community', which is why he instead wrote *The Politics of Friendship*, and spoke of friendship rather than fraternity.

What is your relation to the question of belonging?

ALAIN BADIOU: You know, 'belonging' is a very complicated word for me, because the foundational ontological relation, precisely what is called 'belonging', is ultimately a set that can contain any multiplicity whatsoever, and is defined solely by what belongs to it. But although the relation of belonging is fundamental, it is not the regime of truths, it is the regime of being. That is to say that, after all, it is exactly right, it is indisputable, to say that we are born into systems of belonging.

After all, the symbolic order that constitutes the individual – I won't say the subject, because that would be equivocal – the symbolic construction of the individual can be formulated in terms of identity, in terms of belonging, in terms of kinship, etc., there's no doubt about this.

My problem is therefore not one of saying that belonging is in itself a negative category, because that would be absolutely nihilistic; it would be destructive of things that are, quite obviously, significantly constitutive for individuals, for groups, and for societies. But, on the other hand, what I do insist upon is that there exists in my lexicon, under the name of truths, things that are irreducible to the relation of belonging, and to the community associated with that belonging. What

I mean to say is that there exist things that are diagonal to the system of identities and which, within the system, bring about the possibility of a universality, of something that subtracts itself from the power of communities, identities, and belonging – without for all that destroying them, since they continue to generate the normal continuity of the worldly system within which they act.

What I am really against is making identities, belongings, or communities into normative categories. For me they are not normative categories, they are categories of the construction of what there is qua pure and simple figure of the 'there is'. There is community, there is belonging, there is kinship, there are languages, there are countries. Yes, there are!

What interests me in life is the moment when life can touch, not upon what there is, but precisely upon what is not there in this 'there is'. And what is not there in this 'there is' is nevertheless not something external to it, but something that can be made with the 'there is', by freeing oneself from its borders, its limits, making crossings and diagonals, precisely with a universal signification.

For, although it is always born in a real and symbolic context constituted of belongings and identities, it turns out that it creates something that is not reducible to, does not work within, does not fit into the closure of its identities.

I hold very strongly to this point, to what seems like its most conservative part, the part that says: it is senseless to declare that we're going to destroy identities. I think this is a maximalist thesis, and ultimately a very dangerous one, since, as we know, the idea of destroying one identity can very well conceal the affirmation of some other identity.

After all, we could say that Hitler, also, wanted the Aryans to affirm themselves in that way, as something superior to all other identities. And, being superior to all other identities, he held that the mass murder of an identity he considered as an immanent threat was the only way to achieve this exit from identity. So, I repeat, there are and always will be identities.

The vision here is not that we are going to undo identities, belongings, communities, but simply that the elements of subjective construction we will favour are those that are irreducible to the existing fabric of belongings, though they do not exclude them.

Giovanbattista Tusa: To think politics, after a *mortal* crisis of Marxism, which, not yet dead, was in fact historically destroyed, demanded precisely that one remain 'in a position of immanence to this crisis'.[32] The end of classical Marxism and therefore the end of classes, the end of their opposition.

All political referents having disappeared, in the sense that, as you wrote some time ago, once '[w]ith regard to Marxism, the political references endowed with real working-class and popular life today are all atypical, delocalized, errant', it only remained to abide in the 'uninhabitable place of a Marxist heterodoxy that is to come'.[33]

I know that you're not fond of the rhetoric of death, or incessant calls to finitude. Yet, as you ask in 'Of an Obscure Disaster', wouldn't the evocation of death in relation to communism 'lead us to a suitable nomination for that of which we are the witnesses'?[34]

Alain Badiou: Yes, I now realize, looking at this whole problem again, that when I said that Marxism was probably in a mortal crisis, I was basically talking about a certain brand of Marxism. I was talking about Marxism as a cultural phenomenon, shared by everyone, with its own system of historical references.

I was essentially talking about Marxism in the sense in which Sartre said that Marxism was the unsurpassable horizon of our culture. Sartre said it: Marxism is the unsurpassable horizon of our culture. And it's clear to me that he was talking about Marxism in so far as Marxism was omnipresent – whether one was for or against it, it was there. And it was there in a twofold way. It was there because there were socialist states, but it was also there in the figure of a potential, a force, an established force in the world. And it was also there as one of the century's great modes of thought, a fundamental choice, etc. So, it was a presence, it had a great presence, impressive, material, national, state, etc. It also had a great spiritual presence; that was what Marxism was.

And when I said that there was a mortal crisis, I meant that all of this, there is a good chance that, at some point, it will no longer exist, and indeed, I think that today it no longer exists. In this form, Marxism no longer exists. The socialist states are gone, along with any evidence of a Marxist culture, in differing states of health but present everywhere. So, there was indeed a mortal crisis of this particular Marxism, Marxism as an unsurpassable cultural horizon.

The conclusion that I draw from this today is that we must resuscitate Marxism, but not that Marxism: as always, the resurrection is never in fact a resurrection of exactly the same thing. We must resuscitate the Marxism that we need today. And this Marxism will inevitably be resuscitated.

Why? Because the hegemonic ideology today is liberalism. Which means that we have gone back to something like the years 1830–1840, that is to say we are in a moment when capitalism is conscious of its victory. In 1840, it was consciousness of its birth, of the enormous space that had opened up for it. Today it is consciousness of its victory. Which is not the same thing, but it has finally overcome the test, the test of the former Marxist hegemony, and has become established.

And in the end we will rediscover, in a strange kind of way, at a very general level, the contradiction between liberalism and communism, the contradiction that structured the revolutionary and workers' movements throughout the whole of the nineteenth century. We will come back to it in terms which are not yet fixed, which are still uncertain, in search of themselves. But it is obvious that it is a matter of a new Marxism. The name 'Marxism' itself will reappear. And communism will reappear along with it. And this in an inevitable confrontation with liberalism. In regard to which, I still insist on the fact that, in my view, there is no such thing as neo-liberalism.

There is nothing new about what we're being told today. It is truly the original capitalist dogma. It is competition as absolute law, and the concentration of capital on an unprecedented scale. All of the great laws of elementary Marxism are especially visible and active today. Which makes it all the more strange that Marxism itself is not there. On the contrary, what it described is there, more than ever: the internationalization of capital, the world market, the concentration of capital, and even something we long believed was not quite right, namely the complete penetration of capitalism into the rural zones, into agricultural production. This, also, is really taking place on a planetary scale now.

So, this is why I think it is true that there has been a mortal crisis of Marxism, but it is no less true that there will be a resurrection, in conditions that I cannot really predict but which I believe to be ineluctable. It will take place once more in a kind of arduous close combat, at first dominated by the reappearance as such of liberal ideology as the hegemonic and even the only ideology of societies in today's world.

GIOVANBATTISTA TUSA: From the disaster to the event. The renunciation of the obscure fascination for catastrophes, the ecstasy of destruction, the revelatory pedagogy expressed in that which does not seem reducible to thought, seems to me to be one of the founding themes of your work.

You have long emphasized that the twentieth century was the century of the 'unreconciled', the century that 'thought itself simultaneously as end, exhaustion, decadence *and* as absolute commencement'.[35]

But the twenty-first century seems to have begun under the sign of the incomprehensible catastrophe, the systemic crisis, and the virtuous inhuman war.

Even revolutions themselves, we might say, seem to be drawn towards this catastrophe without any possibility of comprehension of which Hannah Arendt spoke in *What is Politics?*: Wars 'are monstrous catastrophes that can transform the world into a desert and the earth into lifeless matter', and all that 'revolutions – if we seriously regard them with Marx as the "locomotives of history" – have demonstrated with any clarity is that this train of history is evidently hurtling towards an abyss, and that revolutions, far from being able to avert calamity, only frighteningly accelerate the speed with which it unfolds.'[36]

What of revolutions today, then?

ALAIN BADIOU: I would say that we are in an uncertain period but, in my view, a period that even so, in its own way, can be assured of a resurrection of Marxism – this is the first point. In a struggle against a reconstituted liberalism, it is certain that the category of revolution must be re-examined, and will be re-examined, as a part of the resurrection of Marxism, probably with an entirely new extension and signification.

Among other things, the nature of that which, from the point of view of politics, can be considered as an 'event' will be called into question, because 'revolution' has also been the name of those major political events that humanity has been capable of seizing. But so long as this remains articulated around the entirely different category of power, something will remain dysfunctional.

So, what is to become of the category of revolution in all this? That was your question. In this matter, on the contrary, I am in a time of great uncertainty, because I still think that the experience of real socialism was also an experience that belongs in the category of revolution.

The socialist states came about as a result of revolutionary processes, in an organized insurrectional form in the case of the Bolshevik revolution, in the most unprecedented form of the protracted war based in the countryside in the case of China. But both cases involved militarized processes for the overthrow of established state power, considered as a class power, and its replacement by something like what Marx called the dictatorship of the proletariat. Here we have a classic enough schema, and it must obviously be reinterrogated from the point of view of the question of the state.

Why? Because today we are clearly aware that the ultimate failure of the socialist countries was down to the hypertrophy of the state and the conviction that the state was the absolute key to the transformation of the social world, and of humanity in general. In other words, it was thought that the instrument that had produced the revolutionary victory as such was also the instrument that could direct and organize the new society. I think that it was historically demonstrated that this is not the case, even if the methods used to resolve the problem of victorious insurrection, namely the centralized party and the hierarchical and military organization of the party and then of the state – since the party and the state were fused – had resolved the problem from a certain point of view.

There have been victorious revolutions, there's no doubt about that – but that hasn't resolved the problem of communism at all, that is to say the problem of the strategic aim of the new political configuration. Instead, the movement was towards an extremely hierarchized economism of the state, and a terrorist politics – which was therefore ultimately an annihilation of politics. There was a depoliticization in favour of the absolute sovereignty of the state, a development that was really completely unforeseen within the framework of classical Marxism.

So, what does it mean to say revolution today? It's truly an open question, because 'revolution' today must mean, to put it entirely abstractly, a figure of collective and social mobilization moving in the direction of communism.

We can no longer simply say that 'revolution' is a question of power. Yes, it's a question of power, but we know that the question of power is ultimately not, in and of itself, strategically determinative.

If we are to retain the word, then, we must conceive of 'revolution' as having a substantially different meaning to the one it had throughout the nineteenth and the first half of the twentieth century. And indeed, whatever you may think of them, there have been anticipations of this. From this point of view, Trotsky was probably not completely wrong when he talked about permanent revolution, and the Chinese were not wrong to coin the peculiar expression 'cultural revolution'.

As we can see, what we are looking for is a reactivation of the word 'revolution', in conditions which are no longer simply those of the violent overthrow of a hostile power, but which go in the direction of the effective construction of a society that will move beyond socialism towards communism, or will orient itself towards the sovereignty of the common good, as in the original definition of communism.

GIOVANBATTISTA TUSA: In 1967, in a conversation with Jean Duflot later published in *Le rêve du centaure*, Pasolini describes a plan for a film about Saint Paul.

Pasolini transposes the story of Paul into the present: from Damascus (Barcelona), Paul, a Pharisee from a Roman Jewish family, crosses the desert, which in Pasolini's version becomes the roads of Europe, and '[i]n any of these grand streets full of traffic and the usual acts of everyday life, but lost in the most total silence – Paul is seized by light. He falls, and hears the voice of his call.'[37] Thus begins his preaching, which comes to an end after various adventures in New York, the corrupt Rome of the present, where we see the state of injustice that dominates in a slave society such as imperial Rome reflected 'in racism and the condition of Blacks',[38] and where Paul will be martyred.

The contradiction between 'actuality' and 'saintliness' fascinates Pasolini, the opposition between 'the world of history, which tends, in its excess of presence and urgency, to escape into mystery, into abstraction, into unalloyed interrogatives – and the world of the divine, which, in its religious abstractness, on the contrary, descends among men, becoming concrete and effective'.[39]

The saintliness of Saint Paul was a rupture in which the novelty of speech, although totally immersed in the present, broke with all contingencies, with all factual states of affairs. How singular, in this sense, is the obstinacy that Pasolini attributes to Paul in his script for the unrealized film.

In its transposition into the present, Paul's speech, reconstructed, as Pasolini says, 'by analogy', has nothing actual about it, and remains 'the other face': the inactual, that which at every instant modifies the present, never allowing it to remain identical to itself.

In referring to Saint Paul, you again turn to a figure of militancy driven by individual obstinacy. And yet you recall how the French Revolution replaced the individual aristocratic figure of the warrior with the democratic and collective figure of the soldier, creating a new imaginary for the relation between human and inhuman. 'The great notion was the "mass uprising"', you write, 'the mobilization of the revolutionary people, regardless of their condition, against the common enemy.'[40]

A. BADIOU AND G. TUSA

If, therefore, the soldier was the modern symbol of the capacity of human animals to create something beyond their own limits, thus to participate in the creation of eternal truths, what new imaginary is possible now for a collective creation, what figure?

ALAIN BADIOU: You're entirely right to say that it is in the context of an antagonistic binary that the classical figure of heroism is born. Heroism is always heightened when the enemy is identified simply and univocally and the figure of the hero is the figure of he who incarnates most fully the internalization of conflict as such, at the risk of his life, at the risk of failure.

I think that the individual and often sacrificial heroism of the binary is replaced by something else that may be a heroism in its own way, but a heroism that creates an extremely complex movement in which one could, in a certain sense, be a hero of the State, a hero of the organization, a hero of the masses. These are three entirely different forms of heroism that will circulate in collective creation.

It's important to see that those who were revolutionary heroes have found it very difficult to be

heroes of the state. For example, from the nine-
teen twenties onward Lenin was overwhelmed
by anxiety, uncertainty, criticism, and we have
from him very violent texts where he says that
ultimately, all they have done is to reinstate a
disgusting bureaucracy. Basically, Lenin didn't
really know what to do – that's the problem –
and, in effect, he proposes a collective hero when
he says: What we need is to have a workers' and
peasants' inspectorate who come to see exactly
what happens in the offices. Finally, there it is
– and then he died. In a certain sense, it was the
same with Mao.

We can see well enough that at a certain point
he becomes absolutely exasperated by how things
are going, and will end up throwing himself into
some dreadful and extremely costly adventures
because, the longer he goes on, the more he
becomes sidelined. And this, I think, is an indi-
cation of the fact that the category of revolution
produces its own workforce. But this workforce
has no future. Trotsky tells us that, one day,
during the revolutionary years, someone asked
him: But who is this Stalin we see everywhere?
And he answered: Stalin is the most mediocre
figure in our political leadership. Which was true.

There is a tactical mediocrity which is not at all that of revolutionary heroism.

GIOVANBATTISTA TUSA: As you have written, what you dub 'democratic materialism' presents as an objective given, or an inevitable outcome of historical experience, what is called the 'end of ideologies'. But as you observe bitterly in *Logics of Worlds*, in reality this amounts to a violent subjective injunction, the real content of which is: 'Live without Idea.'

Over the course of the last two centuries, in Western societies (and beyond) new privileges have been acquired, new expectations and needs have been created, doing away with the idea of an ineluctable destiny; new concepts such as 'dignity' and human 'rights' have become common currency, expectations of equality have been raised. But, at the same time, twenty-four hours a day, every day, inequality is broadcast on television, mass media, and the Internet to every inhabitant of the planet. Which is the reason why, with every step forward, human delusion has increased.

Kill yourself. The *kamikaze*. Here perhaps is the extreme figure of negation, of radical loss, the figure that silences democratic reason, the agora of opinions on the best or the least worst. The figure of the terrorist was originally, neutrally, someone involved in *The Terror*. And indeed, the Jacobins officially declared themselves terrorists.

Of course, we should also cite the different types of 'terrorism' of which French anti-Nazi militias or the Italian resistance were accused. Not to mention, of course, the various 'terrorist' enemies of America who have struggled to liberate their countries from North American imperialism. Today, however, it seems that terrorism is no longer a neutral term, indicating a type of struggle that employs terror as a means of avoiding defeat when faced with a far more powerful enemy.

As we were saying, philosophy, and even reasoning, is supposed to say nothing when faced with this terrorism, defined as overtly 'nihilist' (which is how the Russian terrorism of the nineteenth century anarchists was defined, or defined itself). But isn't it precisely the duty of philosophy to begin when wisdom has finished with all its justifications and its arguments?

Citing *Phaedrus*, in a lecture given just after the murderous attacks that took place in Paris in November 2015, you discuss a moment in Racine's tragedy when Phaedrus, obliged to admit her love which, to her own eyes, is criminal, says: 'My wound is not so recent.' You then add: 'We, also, can say that our wound is not so recent as immigration, as Islam, as the devastation of the Middle East, as Africa being subjected to pillaging. . . .'[41] Alain, where does our wound come from?

ALAIN BADIOU: As you know, and here our final question comes back to the first one, Heidegger – although he was not the first to do so – characterized our time as the time of nihilism. This question of nihilism is a question that looms in philosophy but also in society itself.

I believe that we must indeed understand that what enables nihilism today is in fact capitalist globalization. Because capitalist globalization, in reality, prescribes no objective for human life other than to integrate into this globalization. It is a tautological prescription, because it is a matter of nothing other than maintaining and participating in what is already there – which, what's more, is seen as an irreversible victory or even, by some, as the terminal point of history.

This motif was introduced precisely in relation to globalized capitalism. Today, all subjectivities are convoked in relation to this situation. And the clearest split is between two possible positions.

The first position is to accept one's incorporation into globalized capitalism, at the best level if possible. This level is represented by the category of the West in general, that is to say, properly speaking, by liberal societies with modes of life that allow people to do what they want according to a certain order of ideas – sexual liberation, recognition of minorities, parliaments, elections, all of that. Integration into this, what I call 'desire for the West', is very widespread. We mustn't deceive ourselves about this. Desire for the West, namely the idea that there is no other aim in the world than to find a place, the best place possible, within this assemblage, that of globalized capitalism, is a subjectivity with great force.

The second subjective figure – the one for which this question is central – consists in being gripped by disappointment, by the nihilist bitterness of those who haven't really found that kind of place, or who have reason to think they never will have, or who feel they are excluded

81

from this type of place, and therefore cling on to
. . . on to what? They cling on to precisely what
globalized capitalism devalues and leaves behind,
namely identities. So, they cling on to this negative drive to identity; and for historical reasons,
one of the most active identities is Islamic identity, which, in its historical depth, is basically
the idea of a revenge of the Arab world against a
great defeat that was really suffered, around the
fifteenth century. Then this identitarian – that is
to say absolutely reactive – idea becomes a form
taken on by something more profound, namely
the real or fictional impossibility of finding an
acceptable place.

And the third figure is the figure that opposes
itself to global capitalism's claim to be the law of
the world today. It is a subjectivity that must root
itself in the possibility that there is something
other than this.

So, this sums up everything we've discussed
already: the resurrection of Marxism, a fundamental programme directed against private
property, the rehabilitation of the communist
hypothesis, a new type of militancy, etc. That
is to say, precisely, the proposing of an Idea.
Something which, in the global arena, will be

fostered by the reconstruction of a heterogeneous strategic idea, in conflict with global capitalism's claim to be the only possible form of collective organization.

This is why there is so much debate around the Idea, the life without Idea, what is an Idea, etc. It is because this gives the impression of a return to idealism. It gives the impression that today materialism is really on the side of globalized capitalism and that idealism is situated on the side of revolutionaries, who were traditionally materialist. But this just proves that the problem has been badly posed.

By 'Idea', what I mean, quite simply, is the restitution, as soon as possible, of a non-uniform space. The Idea is that which indicates how there can be a division of possibilities according to norms that are not unified. In this case, on the political plane, that means reconstructing in one way or another the canonical opposition between communism and capitalism, at the obvious level of ideological stratification, but also at the level of actual specific situations and a programme to transform them, and also at the level of movements. That is the practical content, the effective content, of politics.

I think we have to start from the fact that the current domination of globalized capitalism, with its imperative 'Live without Idea', is a deadly proposition, and that the attacks lend visibility to this deadly dimension. In them, the death becomes visible. The death that is visible, those young people who think that, in the world as it is, their lives are of no importance, but that death can have some importance, because after all it is death that finally shows, that finally reveals – violently, theatrically, tragically – that our world is a world of death.

The death of what, though? The death of that which is not the pure and simple blind, competitive search for a decent place in the world as it is. So, it is death in the sense of the death of everything that might depend on a possibility created by the event, by fidelity, by subjectivation.

We must assume as fact that the murderous activity of vengeful nihilism, clinging to identities, is only a sub-product of the more fundamental nihilism that is the nihilism of capitalism itself.

And yet it is remarkable that those groups who effectively assume the primacy of the death drive, groups of suicide killers – those for whom the life of others, and their own life, means nothing – have never in any way called capitalism itself into question. What's more, the organizations behind them, the people who manipulate all these young men who are sacrificed, absolutely sacrificed, are themselves fully integrated into the world market.

The organization Daesh sells huge quantities of petrol to Turkey. The oil wells of Mosul are still flowing . . . . These are people for whom, as for the vast majority of others, capitalism is the economy's natural form of existence. Therefore, that deadly nihilism stands only in a relative opposition to the desire for the West. It is in fact a relative opposition. We might say that, in reality, desire for the West and the sphere of so-called Islamic terrorism make up, together, the very form of the contemporary world.

There is a conflictual unity of the world, which is the unity of its nihilism. We might say that, basically, we have a commercial nihilism, that is to say a nihilism of capitalist competition in its ordinary or civilized form, and then an aggressive form of nihilism directed against the first form, an identitarian, vengeful nihilism. But in the end, all of it is the same world. I think that's very clear, since the war that is taking place between these two worlds also defines the historicity of this world.

It is as if the most pressing task for the West were to do away with these people who are the parasites of its own existence. This is why, when we hear President Hollande say that we are at war, we can see very well that it is a civil war. We can see it straight away. It isn't a war with something really foreign, because the results of it are going to be police raids on people who live here, the stigmatization of social groups, negative views on the issue of refugees, etc.

And why is it a civil war? Because it is absolutely an intra-capitalist war. So, against that, to reactivate the Idea, that is to say to render it present in all the concrete activities of collective life, of organization, of political struggle, of mass movements. To reactivate the Idea is to separate; and this is simply the first stage of a separation from a world governed by a false contradiction.

I will end on this point. The difficulty of the contemporary world is that it continually sets out false contradictions as if they were major antagonistic contradictions. Its propaganda is a propaganda in favour of a desire for the West, against everything which, however much it is really fascinated by the West, gives the appearance of being at war with it. And the idea, the resurrection of Marxism, the relaunching of communism, the figure of new organizations and new popular struggles, all of this serves to organize the figure of a true separation, because all propaganda channels people towards fallacious separations.

Epilogue

God who gives life to the dead and calls into being things that were not.

Saint Paul's Epistle to the Romans, 4:17

GIOVANBATTISTA TUSA: We began with the end. And perhaps, inversely, we will finish by coming back once more to the beginning. The question still seems to be the one posed by Hegel in the *Differenzschrift* of 1801, namely that of whether the end must always be seen as another, ulterior beginning, every time.

At the beginning, then, the greatness of philosophy, as you say in your 1985 *Seminar*, would consist in its interrupting the narrative. And 'Parmenides' would be the name of this interruption, of this fault line opened up in the Greek soil, because, as you say,

> [P]hilosophy demands that it should be possible to interrupt the narrative – the Parmenidean institution tells us so. Certainly, there is in Parmenides something of the poetic narrative, but there is a narrative under the condition that it can be interrupted. Perhaps it will only be interrupted to found another narrative regime, but it will be interrupted.'[1]

Heidegger wrote that Parmenides and Heraclitus are the two thinkers who remain in a unique co-belonging at the beginning of Western thought: 'the passing of the years and centuries has never affected what was thought in the thinking of these two thinkers', he writes. 'We call what thus precedes and determines all history the beginning [*Das Anfängliche*]. Because it does not reside back in a past but lies in advance of what is to come, [. . .] [I]n essential history [*In der wesenhaften Geschichte*], the beginning comes last.'[2]

How to fight against the obsession with the *initial* that infests philosophy, against the founding rage that insists on being maintained intact, untouchable: in which, as Jean-Luc Nancy writes, we recognize the dread that is the '"metaphysical" obsession par excellence [. . .] the worst and most atrocious of the vulgarities of a hatred of self – of the other-in-the-self – by which is recognized the dreary will to be or to make "oneself"'?[3]

You have spoken several times of 'resurrection', in calling 'the eternity of truths' this inviolate availability making it possible for them to be resuscitated and reactivated in worlds heterogeneous to those in which they were created, and crossing over, as such, unknown oceans and obscure millennia. 'It's absolutely necessary', you say, 'that theory be able to account for this migration.'[4]

Resurrection was also at the centre of your work on Saint Paul. The resurrection of Christ, as you remind us, was the simple element, the fabulous trait, or, if you like, the primordial enunciation of Paul's testimony. The resurrection eradicates negativity. Christ, you write, was drawn 'ἐκ νεκρῶν', out of the dead. And '[t]his extraction from the mortal site establishes a point wherein death loses its power. Extraction, subtraction, but not negation.'[5]

Christ, as Paul writes in his *Epistle to the Romans*, being dead for you, is alive for us. Resurrected from the dead, he no longer dies, and death 'no longer has mastery over him' (Romans 6:8).

Is resurrection the negation of death, the negation of the divine and immobile nature that negates or destroys the human, the negation of the human as continuously dying, the human not as living being but as mortal? Or is resurrection instead beyond negation, beyond the power of death?

ALAIN BADIOU: The contemporary world is a world that offers everything to individuals except for a becoming-subject. And in this sense, it can be said that the contemporary world is the idea of the death of the subject as such, in favour of the existence of human animals competing, in conditions of absolute inequality, to divide up the available resources.

So, from this point of view, it is indeed a matter of proposing a resurrection, it is a matter of proposing a resurrection of the subject, or more exactly a resurrection of subjects or, you could say, a resurrection of subjectivity, it being understood that by subjectivity we once again mean the relation to, the touching of, the incorporation into a process of truth.

So, if the great question of today, in the name of a return to Marxism, a reaffirmation of the Idea, a contestation of globalized capitalism – if all this can in a certain sense be described as a resurrection, a resurrection from the subject's deathly state as instituted by the triumph of the competitive market-oriented universe of globalized capitalism, then this resurrection is obviously essentially affirmative. Its essence is not the destruction of death, and its essence is not to bring about the destruction of capitalism, although it may lead in that direction. Its essence is the reappearance of the possibility of being, and of making it possible for the individual to live up to the stature of the subject he is capable of becoming. Because, ultimately, I think that true life is when an individual perceives that he is capable of far more than he thought he was, when he crosses his own internal limits, precisely in terms of creative affirmation and the realization of a collective idea.

Because in every one of his experiences, the individual who is subjectivated, incorporated into the process of a truth, experiences that he is living, that he is living in the joy of being – and that in itself is enough to separate one from the world as it is.

So, I would say, in agreement with certain of Saint Paul's declarations, that there is a thesis of resurrection that is fundamental, a fundamental possibility. We are not doomed to living this life, a largely animal life, that the desire of the West offers us. We can go beyond it. We can resuscitate in ourselves the capacity to be a subject. And when it is resuscitated, in real practices, in effective creations, then we experience that we have moved beyond that elementary animality that is competitive capitalist humanity.

I will therefore finish by citing Spinoza: We feel and know that we are eternal. There you have it. We experience in time, in concrete life, that we are eternal, that is to say that we are beyond the order of precarity and of the pure and simple placement in the universe that is assigned to us. And since such an experience is generally a shared and collective one, we also experience that we can live up to the challenge of alterity, we can live with others, which in truth strengthens the feeling of being alive itself.

Coda

To the End? Of Europe and Philosophy

The difficulty of making a beginning arises immediately, because a beginning (being something
immediate) does make a presupposition, or, rather, it
is itself just that.

> G. W. F. Hegel, *Encyclopedia of Philosophical*
> *Sciences* (1830), §1[1]

Dear Alain Badiou,
In our brief dialogue, the 'end' was evoked from
the very beginning. And certainly not by chance:
as you write polemically in your *Manifesto*, ours is
the epoch in which subjectivity is driven towards
its completion. Consequently, thought can only
complete itself beyond this 'completion'. But the
enigma of our epoch, you write,

against the nostalgic speculations of feudal socialism whose most complete emblem has certainly
been Hitler, resides first in the local maintenance
of the sacred which has been attempted, but also
denied, by the great poets since Hölderlin. And,
second, in the anti-technological, archaistic reac-
tions which continue to secure together under our
very eyes the debris of religion (from the soul supplement to Islamism), messianic politics (including
Marxism), occult sciences (astrology, healing plants,
telepathic messages, tickle and touch group ther-
apy) and all types of pseudo-bonds for which the
syrupy love exalted in songs – loveless, truthless and
encounterless love – constitutes the flaccid universal
matrix.[2]

Thus the *pathos* of completion swallows up
philosophy in a dark vortex; but philosophy
manifested the necessity to 'think *in level terms
with Capital*' rather than ceding 'to vain nostalgia for the sacred, to obsession with Presence. to
the obscure dominance of the poem, to doubt its
own legitimacy'.[3]

World History, according to Hegel, begins
in the East: 'the dawn of spirit is in the East
– where the sun rises'. But 'spirit' only arrives

at its 'sinking'. In Hegel's *Vorlesungen über die Philosophie der Weltgeschichte* a singular movement continually links origin and destination, a to-and-fro between the beginning and the end.

It is 'Europe' that is the 'end' of that History of Hegelian Spirit of which 'Asia' was the primitive debut. And the crisis of philosophy that Edmund Husserl writes of in *The Crisis of the European Sciences* is the crisis of Europe: because philosophy is, from his perspective, essentially 'European'.

The 'European' project and the philosophical project had seemed to be one and the same, to the point where it was impossible to distinguish between the two, at the moment the French Revolution broke out; just as the project of Enlightenment had restored the edifices of Reason brought down by the Lisbon earthquake on the morning of the Catholic festival of All Saints Day, 1 November 1755.[4]

Husserl's crisis of the European sciences, as Derrida reminds us, was a crisis of the spirit: 'The impotence, the becoming-impotent of spirit, that which violently deprives spirit of its potency, is nothing other than the destination (*Entmachtung*) of the European West.'[5]

A crisis is the crisis of a project, and the 'Western' project seems also to have been that of a philosophy which found in this 'West' its own natural, unique site. Even more than that, it had its base in Europe, and precisely in Western Europe.

More and more often, from all sides, and for diverse reasons, we hear of the inevitable end of 'Europe'. And more and more often, in response, or rather *in reaction* to the 'crisis' of the values of belonging to this 'Europe', we hear talk of an exit from Europe. But is this the end of 'Europe'? Or is it the end of a thinking that seems incapable of freeing itself from the 'project', and consequently from the 'crisis of the project'? Is it possible to think beyond the 'crisis', beyond the 'project'?

G. T.

The word 'project' is equivocal. If it designates the messianic vision of a completed world whose value is in some way transcendent, then it is indeed a lost word, a discredited word. If it designates the practical and transformative tension that is unified in an Idea, and which is active here and now, without any programmatic representation of a stabilized future, then it is a term we can accept.

It is certain today that neither Europe nor, more generally, the West, is the site of any project whatsoever. They are sites of maintenance, they are the great Garages of globalized capitalism. They exert their power by ensuring that, across the world, whatever the political forms or religious or national ideology, in any case the principle of the free market is not questioned, and that the zones of pillage, Africa in particular, remain free zones for commercial competition, for the intervention of military powers, and for the circulation of armed bands offering themselves for hire to both of the above.

Moreover, given that they are no longer anything but conservative material powers with no Idea, I think that Europe and the West will sooner or later be forced to stake their life on a third world war, and probably to perish in it, just as Greece perished in the Peloponnesian War, and colonial Europe began to perish in the 1914 war. Let's assume this will be the end of the US, that ultimate avatar of Europe. We will then see the world redistribute itself, between the renaissance of the communist Idea on a world scale – the only tenable project for the survival of humanity in the very long term – and the resistance of younger imperialisms, China no doubt, India . . . . We shall see.

For now, of course, Europe is no more than an empty envelope, of interest to humanity only as a museum, a cultural reservoir with vestiges of the charm of its former planetary vocation. But this is of no great importance: there is everything to play for on the global scale today. This is why any activity of true thinking is immediately internationalist. The proletarians, as Marx said, have no homeland. Today, intellectuals have no homeland, because no strong idea can have a homeland.

A. B.

Afterword

This short 'afterword' for the new edition of my *Conversations with Alain Badiou* was written in August 2018, two years after the original encounter in Paris, in 2016.

In the meantime, Alain finished and is about to publish the third and final part of his monumental *Being and Event*, with the title *L'Immanence des vérités* (*The Immanence of Truths*), which I was fortunate enough to read recently in a close-to-definitive version.

The following pages have no pretence of explaining what was said (and later transcribed) during the encounter behind the *Conversations* – their intention is rather to bring out the same preoccupations that moved me on that occasion, and still do today.

Daniel Heller-Roazen has admirably captured the narrow yet interminable spaces within which what in classical literature was called a 'commentum' moves, a piece of writing that 'stays at every point "with" that upon which it comments [. . .] an eternal accompanist, a permanent resident of the shifting space of being "with" (cum). It lives nowhere if not in company: were it ever forced to be, so to speak, without its "with", it would not be at all' (Heller-Roazen 2007, pp. 79-80).

Lisbon, August 2018
Giovanbattista Tusa

My thanks go to Zakiya Hanafi and Philippe Farah for the linguistic help they provided for the writing of this short essay. They advised me skilfully, without trying to normalize my all too disoriented and idiosyncratic style; that of a foreigner writing in a foreign language.

Afterword: The Infinity of Truths

A Very Short Essay on the End of Ends

Giovanbattista Tusa

I

> After philosophy comes philosophy. But it is altered
> by the after.
>
> Jean-François Lyotard,
'Foreword: After the Words'

If, in his *Seventh Letter*, Plato could confess the
intimate motivations that prompted him to
become directly involved in the political affairs
of Sicily, it is because he somehow felt that in
his own life and thought, the original unity of
theory and praxis had already been lost. 'I sailed
from home', writes Plato, 'in the spirit which
some imagined, but principally through a feeling

of shame with regard to myself, lest I might some day appear to myself wholly and solely a mere man of words, one who would never of his own will lay his hand to any act' (*Letter VII* 328c).[1] Underlying what is considered to be the Western philosophical tradition, there appears to be the realization that a 'before' (Egypt, the gods, Socrates) has been lost: but precisely because of this loss, the lost sense, unexpressed, can finally be problematized, posited, presented.

For Martin Heidegger, philosophy is defined from its very beginnings as the desire to make meaning, and at the same time it binds its destiny to the necessity of a sense that cannot be exhausted in any meaning. In the terminal phase of what Heidegger called metaphysics, the tension that has always inhabited Western thought finally manifests itself by exceeding every attribution of meaning that had been generated until then. In Heidegger's eyes, the contemporary age presents itself as one of widespread unfamiliarity, of universal uprootedness, an age in which the constant process of domesticating the world paradoxically generates uninhabitable places. The end of philosophy announces that, 'in its epigonality and derivativeness', philosophy has reached a limit, a boundary from which it can only turn back upon itself. In Heidegger's view, 'the task of thinking would then be the abandonment of the thinking in force until now so as to determine the proper matter for thinking' in its unprocessed, necessitating force. The return – Heidegger reminds us enigmatically – is to what Plato calls in his Seventh Letter *to pragma auto*, 'the thing itself' (Heidegger 1993a, p. 437).

In the autumn of 1946, during one of the darkest moments of the post-Second World War period in Europe, leading German officials were judged guilty of 'crimes against humanity' by the International Military Tribunal of Nuremberg.[2] That same year, Heidegger composed his 'Letter on "Humanism"' in reply to Jean Beaufret's question to him on how to restore meaning to the word 'humanism', after the events that had shaken the human world during those recent, terrible years.[3]

The word 'humanism' – this is Heidegger's response – should be abandoned. The catastrophe of the present time is actually nothing but the result – the end – of Western humanistic concepts: Christianity, Marxism, existentialism are nothing but organized ways of evading the ultimate question of the essence of human beings. Both in its ancient forms and in its modern ones stemming from the *Aufklärung*, humanism did nothing but elude the human being. To understand 'the being of the human being' Heidegger argues that we must take our distance from the most pernicious of the representations to which the Western metaphysical tradition has accustomed us, which is to say, the idea of the human being as an animal 'augmented' by spiritual elements: an *animal rationale.* Every attempt to understand the decisive factor of *humanitas* in a biological or zoological perspective and to establish an ontological community between human beings and animals must, according to Heidegger, be utterly rejected (Heidegger 1993, p. 227). Beyond or below the Western understanding of what 'human' means – Heidegger recalls while reading Aristotle's *Nicomachean Ethics* (Z 7, 1141b) – philosophers are at home with what is 'excessive, and thus astounding, and thereby difficult, and hence in general "demonic" – but also useless, for they are not seeking what is, according to straightforward popular opinion, good for man' (Heidegger 1992, p. 100). Meditating and caring for what is outside of human's essence, they are connected with what human beings do not have any familiarity with.[4]

Dasein, of which Heidegger writes about since *Being and Time*, has long left the earth of the metaphysical human. Jacques Derrida stresses that in the 'Letter on "Humanism"' the 'magnetic attraction' of that which is the 'property of man' will orient the various paths of Heidegger's thought. 'It is' – as Derrida writes in *The Ends of Man* – 'within the enigma of a certain proximity, a proximity to itself and a proximity to Being that we shall see constituting itself against humanism and against metaphysical anthropologism, another instance and another insistence of man' (Derrida 1969, p. 45). The end of man, concludes Derrida, 'is the thought of Being' in a limiting that re-opens one to the other: 'man is the end of the thought of Being, the end of man is the end of the thought of Being. Man has always been his proper end; that is, the end of what is proper to him. The being has always been its proper end; that is, the end of what is proper to it' (Derrida 1969, p. 55).

The human is to be found in a space of possibility, in a world of organic and non-organic entities, both living and non-living: beasts, plants, stones, gods, temples, fields, sidereal bodies, atmospheres. Instead of seeking truth inside the human being, Heidegger calls upon us to become intimate with the unlimited monstrousness of the external, which no globalization or all-encompassing system of domination of the earth will ever be able to map out. Modern experience disconnects thought from knowledge; it pushes the present to its contemporary extreme, to the transformation of the world beyond its interpretation. If for thousands of years the canonical definition of limit was the one Aristotle gives in his *Metaphysics*, which states that the limit means the furthest part of each thing, the first point outside which no part of a thing can be found, and the first point within which all parts are contained (Aristotle, *Metaphysics* V, 17, 1022 a), then to conceive of the furthest part of the contemporary – to conceive of its extreme – actually means to conceive of that which cannot be circumstantiated. Seen from this perspective, the urgency consists thus in taking meaning to its limit, and in presenting the limit as the sense of the present.

II

This is a war that possesses numerous less esoteric names: The Idea against reality. Freedom against nature. The event against the state of affairs. Truth against opinions. The intensity of life against the insignificance of survival. Equality against equity. Rebellion against tolerance. Eternity against History. Science against technics. Art against culture. Politics against management. Love against the family.

Alain Badiou, 'The Infinite', in *The Century*

For Alain Badiou contemporary philosophy combines 'a deconstruction of its past with an empty wait for its future' (Badiou 2008, p. 4), whereas the singular and irreducible role of philosophy – this is one of Badiou's unwavering thoughts, starting from his earliest philosophical works – is to establish a point of discontinuity within the discourse, an unconditional point. In a paper given in Sydney in 1999, titled 'The Desire of Philosophy and the Contemporary World', Badiou recalled an odd phrase from a poem of Rimbaud that, for him, captures the desire of philosophy:[5] 'les révoltes logiques' – logical revolts. As Badiou explained on that occasion, 'at base the desire of philosophy implies a dimension of *revolt:* there is no philosophy without the discontent of thinking in its confrontation with the world as it is. Yet the desire of philosophy also includes *logic;* that is, a belief in the power of argument and reason' (Badiou 2014, pp. 39–40).

To discern the indiscernible: as early as his *Manifesto*, Badiou was writing that we are no longer forced to choose between the nameable and the unthinkable. Philosophy did not figure out how to think at the height of Capital, he insists in that text, just as it was unable to measure up to the desacralization of the epoch. It has left 'the "Cartesian meditation" incomplete by going astray in the aestheticization of willing and the pathos of completion, the destiny of oblivion and the lost trace', and is thus incapable of saying goodbye, without any nostalgia, to the non-being of the bond and the absoluteness of the multiple. Philosophy has been incapable of understanding – Badiou insists on this more than once – that we have 'entered into a new phase of the doctrine of Truth, that of the multiple-without-one, or of the fragmentary, infinite and indiscernible totalities' (Badiou 1999, p. 58).

In the contemporary epoch, 'nihilism' would consist of a sort of generalized atomism, in which no symbolic guarantee seems capable of standing up to the abstract potency of Capital, which is, for Badiou, the only 'nihilistic' force that has actually implemented a brutal desacralization of the earth.[6] But this desacralization must be welcomed by philosophy, in all its extreme consequences, rather than being moralistically rejected, because it is a 'necessary condition that exposes the pure multiple as the foundation of presentation: it denounces every effect of the One as a simple, precarious configuration'. As he argues in *Manifesto*, it is to the errant automation of Capital that we owe our deliverance 'from the myth of Presence', from 'the guarantee which it grants to the substantiality of the bonds and to the durability of essential relations' (Badiou 1999, p. 57).

In fact, only bodies and languages may exist in the contemporary world. The absolute and universality have become dangerous concepts. The epoch, as Badiou describes it, is permeated with what he recently called the 'ideology of finitude', which is characterized by a triple 'hypostasis of the finite':

First, the finite is what there is, what is. To accept finitude falls within the reality principle, which is a principle of obedience: we have to submit to the realistic constraints of finitude. This is the principle of the objectivity of the finite. Second, the finite determines what can be, what can occur. This is the principle of restriction of the possibilities: the poor and common critique of 'utopias', of 'charitable illusions', of all the 'ideologies' considered to be matrices of a destructive imaginary, whose paradigm in the previous century has been the communist adventure. And third, finitude prescribes what should be, i.e. the ontological form of our duty, which ultimately always comes down to the duty of respecting what there is, that is to say, basically, capitalism and nature. This supposes – and this is indeed an axiom of finitude – that capitalism is fundamentally natural. This is the principle of the authority of the finite.

(Badiou 2018, p. 14)

'Finitude', the central philosophical figure of the past century, doesn't refer to a given fact or condition but to an active relation with the end that is constitutive of the human way of being. Finitude is not taken to be a limitation or a lack as compared with an infinity, but rather as eminently affirmative, as the proper mode of access to being or to meaning. Man only is finite and finitude is his way of being, be it individually or collectively. *Existentialism is a Humanism*, the famous conference by Jean-Paul Sartre from October 1945, in which the French philosopher reiterates that man is condemned – in view of the disasters the world went through in the preceding years – to shape himself and the world, seems to remain, despite the innumerable critiques it was subjected to, the philosophical manifesto of the twentieth century.

III

This takes deep study,
A learning to unlearn
And sequestration in freedom from that convent
Where the poets say the stars are the eternal brothers,
And flowers are penitent nuns who only live a day,
But where stars really aren't anything but stars,
And flowers aren't anything but flowers,
That being why I call them stars and flowers.

Alberto Caeiro, The Keeper of Flocks

In *The Immanence of Truths*, the third part of his *Being and Event*, Alain Badiou goes so far as to accept for his work the definition that Alberto Caeiro, one of the heteronyms of the Portuguese poet Fernando Pessoa, gives of his own thought: a metaphysics without metaphysics (Badiou 2018, p. 191). Poet, anti-philosopher, Alberto Caeiro presents in his poems a peculiar ontology, an ontology of things existing purely, that we can only access through a physics of sensations, gestures and actions. 'This poetry of the naked being', writes Badiou, 'is itself a naked, descriptive poetry that aims at something as rigorous in its simplicity as what exists, nothing but a separate objective proposition, whether we grasp it or not' (Badiou 2018, p. 191).

For Badiou 'the singular line of thought developed by Pessoa is such that none of the established figures of philosophical modernity is capable of sustaining its tension' (Badiou 2004, p. 37): the confrontation with his poetic oeuvre opens up an unexplored space for thought that would allow philosophy to discover new and unexpected horizons of meaning.[7] The singularity of the 'Pessoa event', according to Badiou, is not only beyond the opposition of Platonism and anti-Platonism; it also cuts through transversally the historical philosophical space opened up by this opposition. If Pessoa represents 'a singular challenge for philosophy', 'if his modernity is still *ahead of us*, remaining in many respects unexplored, it is because *his thought-poem inaugurates a path that manages to be neither Platonic nor anti-Platonic*', so that Pessoa poetically defines 'a site for thinking that is truly *subtracted* from the unanimous slogan of the overturning of Platonism'. To this day, concludes Badiou, 'philosophy has yet to comprehend the full extent of this gesture'[8] (Badiou 2004, p. 38).

In Plato's *Republic* the quarrel between philosophy and poetry dates back to very ancient (παλαια), almost immemorial times (*Republic*, 607b). The poem has always 'disconcerted philosophy' (Badiou 2014a, p. 31) but Badiou calls into question Plato's decision to ban the poet from the *polis*, and consequently to eliminate this immemorial conflict between truth and semblance. He argues that this conflict should instead be maintained: the poem and the matheme are, in his view, irreconcilably and constitutively primordial conditions for philosophy. Indeed, in *Conditions* he writes that philosophy can only establish itself 'through the contrasting play of the poem and the matheme, which form its two

primordial conditions (the poem, whose authority it must interrupt; and the matheme, whose
dignity it must promote)'. We might say, continues Badiou, that 'the Platonic relation to the
poem is a (negative) relation of condition, one
that presupposes other conditions (the matheme,
politics, love)' (Badiou 2008, p. 22). The poem
gathers 'the means to think the outside-place
(hors-lieu), or the beyond of any place', which is
to think 'a presence that, far from contradicting
the matheme, also implies "the unique number
that cannot be another"' (Badiou 2008, p. 41).
Matheme and poem are 'the two extremes of
language' (Badiou 2014a, p. 33), because at stake
in both is the destitution of the fetishism of the
object: both the poem and the matheme, in their
pure literal givenness, challenge the primacy of
objectivity. The thought of the poem, according
to Badiou, only begins 'after the complete disob-
jectification of presence': far from being a form
of knowledge, the poem is rather 'a thought that
is obtained in the retreat, or the defection, of
everything that supports the faculty to know'
(Badiou 2014a, p. 31). Poetry is an essential use
of language, says Badiou, not because it is able
to commit language to Presence, but because

it is able to maintain in language 'that which – radically singular, pure action – would otherwise fall back into the nullity of place. Poetry is the stellar assumption of that pure undecidable, against a background of nothingness, that is an action of which one can only *know* whether it has taken place inasmuch as one *bets* upon its truth' (Badiou 2005, p. 192). Seen from this perspective, poetry is revealed as a negative machinery, 'which states being, or the idea, at the very point where the object has vanished' (Badiou 2014a, p. 29).

Badiou finds it particularly significant that Martin Heidegger and Rudolf Carnap, who were divided over everything, nevertheless shared the idea of having reached the end of metaphysics as well as the firm conviction that this 'end' must be inhabited and activated. While Carnap thinks that the scientific operation must be purified, Heidegger believes that the nihilistic manifestation of metaphysics, in its contemporary form of technoscience, must be opposed by a path of thinking modelled on poetry. In other words, both Heidegger and Carnap share the clamorous gesture of an almost complete 'disentanglement' of philosophy and mathematics which is the 'Romantic gesture par excellence'[9] (Badiou 2004a, p. 22).

Badiou's idea is that Romantic speculation 'opposes time and life as temporal ecstasies to the abstract and empty eternity of mathematics' (Badiou 2004a, p. 24), thereby creating a disposition of thinking that considers finitude to be the essence of man, and inscribes in philosophical thought the representation of the limit as a horizon. In his opinion, this is a catastrophic move that must be strenuously opposed: the ontologies of Presence present the limit as the moment when thought is exposed to the critical risk, the moment when thought exposes itself to its own incompleteness and, simultaneously, to its own potency. But mathematical ontology – we read in one of the appendices to *Being and Event* – 'warns us of the contrary' for the limit cardinal, in fact, contains nothing more than that which precedes it. This is 'a teaching of great political value', Badiou stresses emphatically, in that 'it is not the global gathering together "at the limit" that is innovative and complex, it is rather the realization, on the basis of the point at which one finds oneself, of the one-more of a step. Intervention is an instance of the point, not of the place. The limit is a composition, not an intervention' (Badiou 2005, p. 451).

A philosophical act is not only a demarcation, or the revealing of a trace 'at the limit', of a remainder that has been abandoned by Presence or made destitute of its essence. For Badiou, it contains an affirmation of a concrete point, a political imperative, the affirmation of one world. In his *Manifesto for Philosophy*, Badiou wrote that Heidegger's power of persuasion rested in the fact of having captured not only the destitution of the fetishism of the object and the opposition between truth and knowledge, but also and especially 'the essential disorientation of our epoch'. For this reason, the fundamental criticism of Heidegger 'can only be the following one: the Age of Poets is completed, it is *also* necessary to de-suture philosophy from its poetic condition. Which means that it is no longer required today that disobjectivation and disorientation be stated in the poetic metaphor. Disorientation can be *conceptualized*' (Badiou 1999, p. 74).

In this sense, for Badiou, Cantor's theory of transfinite sets was able to realize the desacralization of the infinite, which the materialists had failed to make possible. Until Cantor, in fact, the Infinite 'had been linked to the One in the conceptual form of the God of religions or metaphysical systems', and the consequence of this pernicious and intractable connection was that 'the domain of human thought was the finite, with our being essentially creatures doomed to finitude' (Badiou 2011, p. 113). In his *After Finitude*, Quentin Meillassoux points out that ever since Cantor's revolutionary set theory we know that 'we have no grounds for maintaining that the conceivable is *necessarily* totalizable. For one of the fundamental components of this revolution was the *detotalization of number*, a detotalization also known as *the transfinite*', giving credit to Badiou for having understood and expressed, in *Being and Event*, 'the ontological pertinence of Cantor's theorem, in such a way as to reveal *the mathematical conceivability of the detotalization of being-qua-being*', and for having used mathematics itself 'to effect a liberation from the limits of calculatory reason' (Meillassoux 2009, p. 103).

According to Meillassoux, disorientation of all human thought and being affects the entire sphere of modern thought. The world of Cartesian extension – a world that acquires the independence of a substance and is conceivable as indifferent to everything in it that corresponds to the vital bond we forge with it – is 'this *glacial* world that is revealed to the moderns, a world in which there is no longer any up or down, centre or periphery, nor anything else that might make of it a world designed for humans' (Meillassoux 2009, p. 115). Human beings are no longer capable of investing the world with the meaning that allows them to inhabit it, to make their environment meaningful. The statements of thought are conceived in such a way that they are identical to what they would have been if human thought had never existed to think them. Scientific thought hypothesizes its general capacity to formulate laws – laws belonging to a world without us – irrespective of the question of the existence of a knowing subject. For the first time, concludes Meillassoux, the world manifests itself as capable of subsisting 'without any of those aspects that constitute its concreteness for us' (Meillassoux 2009, pp. 115–16).[10]

IV

We were not seeking a clear separation between life and concept, nor the subordination of existence to the idea or the norm. Instead, we wanted the concept itself to be a journey whose destination we did not necessarily know. The epoch of adventure is, unfortunately, generally followed by an epoch of order. This may be understandable – there was a piratical side to this philosophy [. . .]

Alain Badiou, *The Adventure of French Philosophy.*

At the turn of the new millennium Badiou concluded his famous seminar on the twentieth century that was nearing its end by reminding us that we must start from the inhuman, from the truths 'to which it may happen that we partake'. Inhuman truths, Badiou explains, which force us to 'formalize without anthropologizing', as Foucault wrote – an endeavour underlying both Althusser's attempt to found a 'theoretical antihumanism' and Lacan's radical dehumanization of the True. For Badiou, then, 'on the shores of the new century', the philosophical task 'against the animal humanism that besieges us' is that of 'a *formalized in-humanism*' (Badiou 2007, p. 178).

In the great Leibnizian tableau that *Logics of Worlds* is, Badiou maintains that the contemporary world shapes the individual in such a way that he recognizes nothing but the existence of bodies separated from every form of immortality: an existence that even the art and artists of our age record, track, and reproduce in the unique form of the 'manifestness of bodies, of their desiring and machinic life, their intimacy and their nudity, their embraces and their ordeals. They all adjust the fettered, quartered and soiled body to the fantasy and the dream. They all impose upon the visible the dissection of bodies bombarded by the tumult of the universe' (Badiou 2009, p. 2). The evidence of this world is what Badiou calls democratic materialism, every expression of which is seeped through with the 'dogma of our finitude' (Badiou, 2009, p. 1). Other unthought axioms are needed; other logics, other ways of formalizing need to be invented.[11] For Badiou, the essence of thinking 'always resides in the power of forms': we need 'to safeguard within us the inhumanity of truths against the animal "humanity" of particularisms, needs, profits and blind archaicisms' (Badiou 2007, p. 164).

A truth is eternal, says Badiou, because it is endlessly available, just as it is absolutely inaccessible; and this is its infinity, which consists in its possibility to be reactivated and transmitted even to worlds vastly remote, almost alien to the

one in which it was conceived. Truths are produced with particular materials, but what Badiou
calls the 'eternity' of truths is 'this inviolate availability', which allows them to traverse, 'as such,
unknown oceans and obscure millennia' (Badiou
2011, p. 129). Because truth is not knowledge, but
rather designates a productive dimension of the
real that always acts to disrupt any substantialized
or established knowledge, it has no generality,
but it emerges in a world, as the presentation of
an inexistent multiple that is capable of trans-
forming the transcendental logic of a world, a site
'through which the possibility of the impossible
comes to be'[12] (Badiou 2009, p. 391).

When detached from all forms of esotericism,
from all ties with the divine, truth is identified
instead with the nondescript, the nameless, the
generic. For Badiou, the being of the situation is
its inconsistency, and consequently, the truth of
this being will present itself as 'any multiplicity,
whatsoever, an anonymous part or consistency
reduced to presentation as such, without a
nameable predicate or singularity [. . .]. A truth
is this minimal consistency (a part, a concept-
less immanence) which certifies in the situation
the inconsistency from which its being is made'

(Badiou 1999, p. 107). Philosophy has the entirely unique task of finding new names that will bring into existence the 'unknown world that is only waiting for us because we are waiting for it' (Badiou 2012, p. 64).

Badiou's profound conviction is that we find ourselves today 'in an intervallic period in which the great majority of people do not have a name', in a world that condemns disproportionate and silenced masses of human beings to invisibility, a world in which the 'only name available is "excluded", which is the name of those who have no name'. The vast majority of humanity is condemned to invisibility, it 'counts today for nothing'. 'Excluded' is, for Badiou, the name of those 'who have no name', and 'market' is simply 'the worldly name of what is not a world', the symmetrical counterpart of the excluded (Badiou 2012, p. 64).

Democratic materialism seeks to destroy what is external to it – this is the thesis of *Logics of Worlds* – and to do this 'it begins by dissolving the inhuman into the human, then the human into everyday life, then everyday (or animal) life into the atonicity of the world', erasing almost all traces of the inhuman, each one of its 'infinite consequences', condemning the contemporary world to a 'purely animalistic, pragmatic notion of the human species', because the democratic materialist is 'a fearsome and intolerant enemy of every human – which is to say inhuman – life worthy of the name' (Badiou 2009, p. 511). In *Logics of Worlds* once again, in fierce opposition to the 'watered-down Kant of limits, rights and unknowables', Badiou quotes the emancipatory formula of Mao Tse-tung: 'We will come to know everything that we did not know before' because the political need in a world like today's is to produce 'new forms to shelter the pride of the inhuman' (Badiou 2009, p. 8) – to conceptualize a form of radical dialectical materialism, which is inseparable from a radical transformation of the human, and which assumes the eternal and ideal 'inhumanity which authorizes man to incorporate himself into the present under the sign of the trace of what changes' (Badiou 2009, p. 511).

If finitude is what we must embrace – the fragments of a world that expresses no totality – we embrace it in order to take on the infinite multiplicity of the works 'by means of which the human animal attests that absolute truths, in heterogeneous worlds, can be immanent to its empirical existence'. We do so because – as Badiou writes in *The Immanence of Truths* – we need to construct for our own times,' as did Plato, Descartes or Hegel, a comprehensive thought based on contemporary rational materials in the domains of mathematics, poetics, love, and politics' – materials that shape anew the forms of art, the absolute creative differences of the new world of love, and the politics 'aiming to protect humankind from the anti-egalitarian, belligerent tyranny of the ownership of goods' (Badiou 2018, p. 682).

A demanding, but necessary thought, a thought 'about what in the human existence separates opinions, or waste, from truths, or oeuvre; that which is relative and submissive from that which is absolute and free'. At stake in it is the possibility of a 'true life' for as Badiou concludes, we are capable of creative processes – in the form of an individual or collective work – wherein singularity, universality and absoluteness are dialectically combined' (Badiou 2018, p. 682).

References

Agamben, G. (2002) *Remnants of Auschwitz: The Witness and the Archive*. Trans. D. Heller-Roazen. New York: Zone Books.

Badiou, A. (1999) *Manifesto for Philosophy*. Trans. N. Madarasz. Albany, NY: State University of New York Press.

_____ (2004). *Handbook of Inaesthetics*. Trans. A. Toscano. Stanford, CA: Stanford University Press.

_____ (2004a) *Theoretical Writings*. Trans. and ed. R. Brassier and A. Toscano. London and New York: Continuum.

_____ (2005) *Being and Event*. Trans. O. Feltham. London and New York: Continuum.

_____ (2007) *The century*. Trans., with commentary and notes, A. Toscano. Cambridge, UK: Polity.

_____ (2008) *Conditions*. Trans. S. Corcoran. London and New York: Continuum.

____ (2009) *Logics of Worlds: Being and Event II*, Trans. A. Toscano. London and New York: Continuum.

____ (2011) *Second Manifesto for Philosophy*. Trans. L. Burchill. Cambridge, UK: Polity.

____ (2012) 'The Caesura of Nihilism', lecture presented at the University of Cardiff on 25 May 2002. Now in *The Adventure of French Philosophy*. Trans. and ed. B. Bosteels. London and New York: Verso.

____ (2014) *Infinite Thought: Truth and the Return to Philosophy*. Trans. and ed. O. Feltham and J. Clemens. London and New York: Bloomsbury.

____ (2014a) *The Age of the Poets: And Other Writings on Twentieth-Century Poetry and Prose*. Trans. B. Bosteels. Introduction E. Apter and B. Bosteels. London and New York: Verso.

____ (2018) *L'Immanence des vérités. L'être et l'événement 3*. Paris: Fayard.

Derrida, J. (1969) 'The Ends of Man'. *Philosophy and Phenomenological Research*, Vol. 30, No. 1, pp. 31–57.

Heidegger, M. (1992) *Parmenides*. Trans. A. Schuwer and R. Rojcewicz. Bloomington and Indianapolis: Indiana University Press.

____ (1993) 'Letter on "Humanism"'. In D. F. Krell (ed.) *Basic Writings*. San Francisco: Harper, pp. 217–65.

____ (1993a) 'The End of Philosophy and the Task of Thinking'. In D. F. Krell (ed.) *Basic Writings*. San Francisco: Harper, pp. 427–49.

_____ (2012) *Contributions to Philosophy (Of the Event)*. Trans. R. Rojcewicz and D. Vallega-Neu. Bloomington and Indianapolis: Indiana University Press.

Heller-Roazen, D. (2007) *The Inner Touch: Archeology of a Sensation*. New York: Zone Books.

Lacoue-Labarthe, P., J.-L- Nancy (1988) *The Literary Absolute: The Theory of Literature in German Romanticism*. Trans. P. Barnard and C. Lester. Albany, NY: State University of New York Press.

Meillassoux, Q. (2009) *After Finitude: An Essay on the Necessity of Contingency*. Trans. R. Brassier. First Paperback edition (First published 2008). London: Continuum.

Negarestani, R. (2008) *Cyclonopedia: Complicity with Anonymous Materials*. Melbourne: Re-Press.

Notes

Apologue

1 This initial brief note was written on 17 January 2017, the day after Alain Badiou's last seminar at the Théâtre de la Commune, Aubervilliers, on the occasion of his eightieth birthday. *Giovanbattista Tusa*

2 'The hermit has the city in the background; for me that city remains Italy. Paris is more a symbol of somewhere else rather than an actual elsewhere.' From the interview 'The Situation in 1978', in Italo Calvino, *Hermit in Paris: Autobiographical Writings*, trans. Martin McLaughlin (Boston and New York: Mariner Books, 2014), p. 188.

3 Calvino, *Hermit in Paris*, p. 169.

4 Gilles Deleuze and Félix Guattari, *What is Philosophy?*, trans. Hugh Tomlinson and Graham Burchill (London and New York: Verso, 1994), pp. 99–100.

5 Plato, 'Republic', in *Complete Works*, ed. John M. Cooper (Indianapolis and Cambridge: Hackett, 1999), p. 1199 (592a–b).

6 On this point see Daniel Bensaïd's fine essay, 'Alain Badiou and the Miracle of the Event', in *Think Again: Alain Badiou and the Future of Philosophy*, ed. Peter Hallward (London and New York: Continuum, 2004), pp. 94–105.

7 Alain Badiou, *Le Séminaire – Images du temps présent (2001–2004)* (Paris: Fayard, 2014), p. 168.

8 Alain Badiou, *Ethics*, trans. Peter Hallward (London and New York: Verso, 2001), p. 40.

9 Alain Badiou, *Saint Paul: The Foundation of Universalism*, trans. Ray Brassier (Stanford, CA: Stanford University Press, 2003), p. 66. Badiou also writes in *Ethics*: 'the onset of asceticism is identical to the uncovering of the subject of truth as pure *desire of self* [*de soi*]. The subject must in some sense continue under his own steam, no longer protected by the ambiguities the representing fiction.' Badiou, *Ethics*, p. 56.

10 Badiou, *Ethics*, p. 41.

11 Ibid., p. 69.

12 Ibid.

13 Badiou, *Le Séminaire – Images du temps présent*, p. 317.

14 Alain Badiou, *Conditions*, trans. Steven Corcoran (London and New York: Continuum, 2008), p. 3.

15 Ibid., p. 4.

16 Ibid.
17 Alain Badiou, 'The End of a Beginning: *Tout va bien*', lecture given in Nantes, 14 February 2003, by the invitation of the association La vie est à nous, as part of the retrospective 'Jean-Luc Godard: années politiques'; reprinted in translation in Alain Badiou, *Cinéma*, ed. Antoine de Baecque, trans. Susan Spitzer (Cambridge: Polity, 2013), pp. 242–51: 242.
18 Ibid., p. 250.

Prologue

1 In Badiou's retelling, the escapee, upon exiting the movie theatre, that dark room where images are projected, is '[a]t first [. . .] blinded by the glare of everything and can see nothing of all the things about which we routinely say: "This exists, this is really here." [. . .] He nevertheless tries to get used to the light. Sitting beneath a solitary tree, he's finally able, after many attempts, to make out the shadow cast by the trunk and the dark outline of the foliage, which remind him of the screen from his former world. In a pool of water at the base of a big rock he manages to see the reflection of flowers and grass. From there he eventually gets to the objects themselves. Slowly, he begins to marvel at the shrubs, the pine trees, a lone sheep. Night falls. Lifting his eyes to the sky, he sees the moon and the constellations; he sees Venus rise. Rigid upright on an old tree stump, he watches for the radiant one. It

emerges from out of the last rays and, sinking ever brighter, is engulfed in its turn. Venus! Finally, one morning, he sees the sun, not in the ever-changing waters, or in its purely external reflection, but the sun itself, in and for itself, in its own place. He looks at it, contemplates it, ecstatic that it is the way it is.' Alain Badiou, *Plato's Republic*, trans. Susan Spitzer (Cambridge: Polity, 2012), p. 214.

2 Ibid., p. 216.

3 Martin Heidegger, 'Plato's Doctrine of Truth', in *Pathmarks*, ed. Will McNeill (Cambridge: Cambridge University Press, 1998), p. 177.

4 Alain Badiou, *Second Manifesto for Philosophy*, trans. Louise Burchill (Cambridge: Polity, 2011), p. 106.

5 Ibid., p. 108.

6 Badiou, *Saint Paul*, p. 7.

7 Ibid., p. 54.

The End

1 Trans. David Constantine, in *Selected Poems* (Newcastle Upon Tyne: Bloodaxe Books, 1990).

2 Immanuel Kant, 'The end of all things' (1794), trans. Allen W. Wood, in *Religion and Rational Theology* (Cambridge: Cambridge University Press, 1996), pp. 217–32: 227.

3 G. W. F. Hegel, *Lectures on the History of Philosophy. The Lectures of 1825–26. Volume I: Introduction and Oriental Philosophy*, trans., ed. Robert F. Brown (Oxford: Clarendon Press, 2009), p. 92.

4 Ibid., p. 200.

5 'For Hegel, philosophy has reached its end because it is capable of grasping what is absolute knowledge. For Marx, philosophy, as interpretation of the world, may be replaced by a concrete transformation of this same world. For Nietzsche, negative abstraction represented by the old philosophy must be destroyed to liberate the genuine vital affirmation, the great "Yes!" to all that exists. And the analytical tendency, the metaphysical phrases, which are pure nonsense, must be deconstructed in favour of clear propositions and statements, under the paradigm of modern logic.' Alain Badiou, 'The Enigmatic Relation Between Politics and Philosophy', in *Philosophy for Militants*, trans. Bruno Bosteels (London and New York: Verso, 2012), p. 6.

6 Alain Badiou, *Manifesto for Philosophy*, trans. Norman Madarasz (Albany, NY: State University of New York Press, 1999), p. 31.

7 Ibid., p. 32.

8 Martin Heidegger, *Introduction to Metaphysics*, trans. Gregory Fried and Richard Polt (New Haven, CT and London: Yale University Press, 2014), p. 42.

9 Alain Badiou, *Le Séminaire – Heidegger. L'être 3 – Figure du retrait (1986–1987)* (Paris: Fayard, 2015), p. 55.

10 It seems to me fundamentally important to cite, if only in a footnote, what Badiou has written on the relation between the poem and the event in *Being*

and Event, specifically in relation to Mallarmé: 'If poetry is an essential use of language, it is not because it is able to devote the latter to Presence; on the contrary, it is because it trains language to the paradoxical function of maintaining that which – radically singular, pure action – would otherwise fall back into the nullity of place. Poetry is the stellar assumption of that pure undecidable, against a background of nothingness, that is an action of which one can only know whether it has taken place inasmuch as one *bets* upon its truth'. Alain Badiou, *Being and Event*, trans. Oliver Feltham (London and New York: Continuum, 2005), p. 192.

11 Alain Badiou, *Que pense le poème?* (Caen: Éditions NOUS, 2016), pp. 10–11.

12 'The age of poets has come to a close. This does not mean that things are clearer now, but that the question is that of clarity. Consequently, we must in our turn break with the Heideggerian desire to perpetuate the obscure. Here I mean by "obscure" not obscurantism, but, in truth, the ambition to perpetuate the poem as an instance of the thinking of the times. From this point of view, our jurisdiction falls under the Platonist paradigm of the primacy of the matheme, not the Presocratic paradigm of the splendid, obscure poem'. Badiou, *Le Séminaire – Heidegger*, pp. 134–5.

13 Ibid.

14 Badiou, *Being and Event*, p. 451.

15 Ibid., p. 93.

16 'Ultimately, the problem of the century is to exist in the non-dialectical conjunction of the theme of the end and that of beginning. "Ending" and "beginning" are two terms that, within the century, remain unreconciled.' Alain Badiou, *The Century*, trans. Alberto Toscano (Cambridge: Polity, 2007), p. 37.

17 The lecture was published in Luca Di Blasi, Manuele Gragnolati, Christoph Holzhey (eds.), *The Scandal of Self-Contradiction. Pasolini's Multistable Subjectivities, Traditions, Geographies* (Vienna and Berlin: Turia+Kant, 2012), pp. 269–77.

18 On the question of the 'manifesto', in *The Century* we read the following: 'What is a Manifesto? The question is of special interest to me in that in 1989 I wrote a *Manifesto for Philosophy*. The modern tradition of the manifesto was established in 1848 by Marx's *Manifesto of the Communist Party*. [. . .] The problem, once again, is that of time. The Manifesto is the reconstruction, in an indeterminate future, of that which, being of the order of the act, of a vanishing flash, does not let itself be named in the present. A reconstruction of that to which, taken in the disappearing singularity of its being, no name can be given.' Badiou, *The Century*, pp. 137–8.

19 Alain Badiou, *À la recherche du réel perdu* (Paris, Fayard, 2015), p. 57.

20 Ibid.

21 Badiou, *The Century*, p. 36.

22 Ibid., p. 32.

23 Ibid., p. 132.

24 Ibid., p. 55. 'The passion of the century is the real, but the real is antagonism. That is why the passion of the century – whether it be a question of empires, revolutions, the arts, the sciences, or private life – is nothing other than war. "What is the century?", the century asks itself. And it replies: "The final struggle".' Ibid., p. 38.

25 André Bazin, 'Death Every Afternoon', trans. Mark A. Cohen, in Ivone Margulies (ed.), *Rites of Realism: Essays on Corporeal Cinema* (Durham, NC and London: Duke University Press, 2003), pp. 27–31: 30.

26 Badiou, *À la recherche du réel perdu*, p. 31.

27 Alain Badiou, *Can Politics Be Thought*, trans. B. Bosteels (Durham, NC: Duke University Press, 2018), p. 36.

28 Badiou, *Conditions*, p. 67.

29 Alain Badiou, *Logics of Worlds*, trans. Alberto Toscano (London and New York: Continuum, 2009), p. 377.

30 Badiou, *Being and Event*, p. 192.

31 Alain Badiou, *The Rebirth of History: Times of Riots and Uprisings*, trans. Gregory Elliott (London and New York: Verso, 2012), p. 67.

32 Badiou, *Can Politics Be Thought?*, pp. 60, 61.

33 Ibid., pp. 63, 64. 'To hold steady in Marxism means to occupy a place that is destroyed and, thus,

uninhabitable. I posit that there exists a Marxist subjectivity that inhabits the uninhabitable. With regard to the Marxism that is destroyed, it stands in a position of inside–outside. The topology of politics, which remains to be thought in the place of the uninhabitable, is on the order of a torsion: neither the interiority to the Marxist–Leninist heritage nor the reactive exteriority of anti-Marxism. This relation of torsion is opposed to all the triumphalism of the previous Marxism, with its infallible rectitude of the "just line". The state of the art in political thinking today gives proof only of a twisted relation to its own history.' Ibid., p. 63.

34 Alain Badiou, 'Of an Obscure Disaster: On the End of the Truth of the State', trans. Barbara P. Fulks, *Lacanian Ink* 22 (2003), pp. 75–6.

35 Badiou, *The Century*, p. 31.

36 Hannah Arendt, *The Promise of Politics* (New York: Schocken Books, 2005).

37 Pier Paolo Pasolini, *Saint Paul: A Screenplay*, trans. Elizabeth A. Castelli (London: Verso, 2014), pp. 6–7.

38 Ibid., p. 9. 'The world in which – in our film – Saint Paul lives and works is therefore the world of 1966 or 1967: as a consequence, it is clear that all of the place names need to be displaced. The centre of the modern world – the capital of colonialism and of modern imperialism – the seat of modern power over the rest of the earth – is not any longer, today,

Rome. And if it isn't Rome, what is it? It seems clear to me: New York, along with Washington. In the second place: the cultural, ideological, civil, in its own way religious centre – the sanctuary, that is, of enlightened and intelligent conformism – is no longer Jerusalem, but Paris. The city that is equivalent to the Athens of that moment, then, is in large measure the Rome of today (seen naturally as a city of grand historical but not religious tradition). And Antioch could probably be replaced, by analogy, by London (in so far as it is the capital of an imperial antecedent of American supremacy, just as the Macedonian-Alexandrian empire preceded the Roman empire). The theatre of Saint Paul's travels is, therefore, no longer the Mediterranean basin but the Atlantic.' Ibid., pp. 3–4.

39 Ibid., p. 5.
40 Badiou, 'The Figure of the Soldier', *Philosophy for Militants*, p. 47.
41 Alain Badiou, *Our Wound is Not So Recent*, trans. Robin Mackay (Cambridge: Polity, 2016), p. 72.

Epilogue

1 Alain Badiou, *Le Séminaire – Parménide. L'être 1 – Figure ontologique (1985)* (Paris: Fayard, 2014), pp. 258–9.
2 Martin Heidegger, *Parmenides*, trans. André Schuwer and Richard Rojcewicz (Bloomington and Indianapolis: Indiana University Press, 1992), p. 1.

3 Jean-Luc Nancy, *The Banality of Heidegger*, trans. Jeff Fort (New York: Fordham University Press, 2017), p. 47. On Heidegger's *Black Notebooks* Jean-Luc Nancy writes: '[I]t is indeed through the self-suppression of the groundless that the victory "of History over the historyless" can arrive [. . .] It was therefore necessary that the agent of Western destruction destroy itself. It is to this that the historico-destinal logic leads according to which beyng was destined in its first beginning towards the advent of another, the true (re)beginning in which it will be given to beyng to make use of beings and no longer to be covered over by them. One is left speechless.' Ibid., p. 51.

4 Badiou, *Second Manifesto for Philosophy*, p. 129.

5 Badiou, *Saint Paul*, p. 73.

Coda

1 G. W. F. Hegel, *The Encyclopedia Logic*, trans. T. F. Geraets, W. A. Suchtig, H. S. Harris (Indianapolis and Cambridge: Hackett, 1991).

2 Badiou, *Manifesto for Philosophy*, p. 57.

3 Ibid., p. 58.

4 'The earthquake of Lisbon sufficed to cure Voltaire of the theodicy of Leibniz', as Adorno writes in *Negative Dialectics,* in 1966.

5 Jacques Derrida, *The Other Heading: Reflections on Today's Europe*, trans. Pascale-Anne Brault and Michael B. Naas (Bloomington and Indianapolis: Indiana University Press, 1992), p. 34.

Afterword

1 It is said that Plato wrote his Seventh Letter in 354 BC to a group of political leaders in Sicily who were allies of Dion, the ruler assassinated not long before. But the letter is also a reflection on questions of a more general nature about philosophy and politics, especially about when a philosopher should become involved in politics. We are of course aware of the interminable discussion on the authenticity of the Platonic letters. Let us accept their authenticity here as a fantastic assumption, an element of narrative fiction.

2 Despite the fact that the phrase 'crimes against humanity' was first employed internationally in a 1915 declaration by the governments of Great Britain, France and Russia, which condemned the Turkish government for the alleged massacres of Armenians as 'crimes against humanity and civilization for which all the members of the Turkish Government will be held responsible together with its agents implicated in the massacres', the first prosecutions for crimes against humanity took place after the Second World War before the International Military Tribunal at Nuremberg.

3 The 'Letter on "Humanism"' was written in response to a letter addressed to Heidegger by Jean Beaufret, with regard to Sartre's lecture at Club Maintenant in Paris, on 29 October 1945, which was published in 1946 as *Existentialism is a Humanism* by Les Éditions

Nagel. Heidegger's letter, originally completed in December 1946, was expanded into an essay and published the following year.

4 The intended readers of Heidegger's *Letter* are not his contemporaries. The missive seems directed rather to those 'Future Ones' (*Die Zukünftigen*), whom we read about in the enigmatic reflections that make up his *Contributions to Philosophy*: a community of strangers, who have intimacy with what usually remains the most inaccessible, 'the stillest witnesses to the stillest stillness in which an imperceptible impetus turns truth out of the confusion of all calculatively correct findings and back into its essence, such that there is kept concealed what is most concealed' (Heidegger 2012, p. 313).

5 Oliver Feltham and Justin Clemens, translating the paper (published with the title 'Philosophy and Desire' in Badiou's collection of essays *Infinite Thought. Truth and the Return of Philosophy*), underline the ambiguity, in French, of the phrase 'le désir de la philosophie'. They highlight: 'in the objective sense of the genitive, it is philosophy which is desired. However, in the subjective sense, it can also be said that it is philosophy which desires, or that there is a desire which traverses philosophy' (Badiou 2014, p. 45).

6 'Capital is the general dissolvent of sacralizing representations, which postulate the existence of intrinsic and essential relations (between man and nature,

147

men, groups and the Polis, mortal and eternal life, etc.)' (Badiou 1999, p. 56).

7 In the musings of his earlier short text 'A Philosophical Task: To Be Contemporaries of Pessoa', Alain Badiou had written that Pessoa's heteronymy can be seen as 'a *dispositif* for thinking, rather than as a subjective drama' (Badiou 2004, p. 43). To be 'contemporaries' of Pessoa is a philosophical task of philosophy because philosophy 'is not – at least not *yet* – under the condition of Pessoa' (Badiou 2004, p. 36). Giorgio Agamben claims, in his *Remnants of Auschwitz*, that 'in twentieth-century poetry, Pessoa's letter on heteronyms constitutes perhaps the most impressive document of desubjectification, the transformation of the poet into a pure "experimentation ground", and its possible implications for ethics' (Agamben 2002, p. 117).

8 'As a temporary definition of philosophical modernity, let us take Nietzsche's slogan, later adopted by Deleuze: to overturn Platonism. Let us then say with Nietzsche that the century's entire effort is "to be cured of the sickness of Plato". It is beyond doubt that this slogan organizes a convergence of the disparate tendencies within contemporary philosophy. Anti-Platonism is, strictly speaking, the *commonplace* of our epoch' (Badiou 2004, p. 37).

9 Philippe Lacoue-Labarthe and Jean-Luc Nancy had underlined in a powerful way the contemporary relevance of romanticism in *The Literary Absolute*. In

their view, although the present period obstinately denies this belonging 'which defines us', nevertheless a 'veritable romantic *unconscious* is discernible today, in most of the central motifs of our "modernity"'. The motif of 'romanticism', they continue, could be found 'in fundamental revolt against Reason and the State, against the totalitarianism of Cogito and System. A romanticism of libertarian and literary rebellion, literary because libertarian, whose art would incarnate insurrection. [. . .] For the literary Absolute aggravates and radicalizes the thinking of totality and the Subject. It *infinitizes* this thinking, and therein, precisely, rests its ambiguity' (Lacoue-Labarthe and Nancy 1988, p. 15).

10 The radical notion that we do not open ourselves up to this world but, rather, it opens us up, butchering us in the process, comes from the Iranian philosopher and writer Reza Negarestani. In his theoretical-fiction novel *Cyclonopedia: Complicity with Anonymous Materials*, radical openness amounts to that which subverts the logic of capacity from within. 'Openness', Negarestani writes, 'emerges as radical butchery from within and without. If the anatomist cuts from top to bottom so as to examine the body hierarchically as a transcendental dissection, then the katatomy of openness does not cut anatomically or penetrate structurally (performing the logic of strata); it butchers open in all directions [. . .]. Openness is not the anthropomorphic desire

to be open, it is the being opened eventuated by the act of opening itself' (Negarestani 2008, p. 203).

11 'There is no doubt whatsoever concerning the existence of truths, which are not bodies, languages, or combinations of the two. And this evidence is materialist, since it does not require any splitting of worlds, any intelligible place, any "height". In our worlds, such as they are, truths advance. These truths are incorporeal bodies, languages devoid of meaning, generic infinites, unconditioned supplements' (Badiou 2009, p. 4).

12 Further on Badiou adds that 'The laws of being immediately close up again on what tries to except itself from them. Self-belonging annuls itself as soon as it is forced, as soon as it happens. A site is a vanishing term: it appears only in order to disappear. The problem is to register its consequences in appearing' (Badiou 2009, p. 391).